# Christmas
## Kindling

A Collection of
Inspiring Stories
to Spark the
Christmas Spirit

# David A. Jacinto

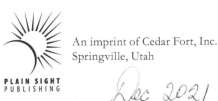

**PLAIN SIGHT**
**PUBLISHING**

An imprint of Cedar Fort, Inc.
Springville, Utah

*Dec 2021*

ISBN 13: 978-1-4621-2321-6

Published by Plain Sight Publishing, an imprint of Cedar Fort, Inc.
2373 W. 700 S., Springville, UT 84663
Distributed by Cedar Fort, Inc., www.cedarfort.com

LIBRARY OF CONGRESS CATALOGING-IN-PUBLICATION DATA

Names: Jacinto, David, 1949- author.
Title: The Christmas kindling: A collection of inspiring stories to spark the
   Christmas spirit / by David Jacinto.
Description: Springville, Utah : Plain Sight Publishing, An imprint of Cedar
   Fort, Inc., [2018] | Includes bibliographical references and index.
Identifiers: LCCN 2018026598 | ISBN 9781462123216 (perfect bound : alk. paper)
Subjects: LCSH: Christmas stories, American. | LCGFT: Short stories.
Classification: LCC PS648.C45 C4488 2018 | DDC 813/.0108334--dc23
LC record available at https://lccn.loc.gov/2018026598

Cover design by Wes Wheeler
Cover design © 2018 Cedar Fort, Inc.
Edited by Kathryn Watkins and Melissa Caldwell
Typeset by Kaitlin Barwick

Printed in the United States of America

10  9  8  7  6  5  4  3  2  1

Printed on acid-free paper

This book is dedicated to my family: my wife, Anne;
my near-perfect children, Michael, Paul, Daniel, and Rachel,
and their wives, Sandra, Elizabeth, Christie, and husband, Jason;
as well as all my perfect grandchildren.

# Contents

# Introduction

*S*cientists tell us there is a trace of gold in everybody. Some say that "the greatest concentration can be found in the human heart." Unfortunately, few have either the patience or perseverance to unearth this precious treasure, but something in the Christmas season seems to change all that. It's the one time of year when we seem to recognize the world is but a looking glass, reflecting back on us the kindness and charity we show our fellow man. The spirit of Christmas often rests in simple acts of service; in simple words or looks; in things so slight and insignificant it's impossible to count them in dollars or cents. Simple gifts may cost little, or even no money at all, yet the happiness and blessings these kindnesses give can sometimes make all the difference, as great as if they cost a fortune. This is a book of stories on the power of the spirit of Christmas—the power to render us happy or unhappy, to make our time on earth light or burdensome, a pleasure or toil.

Happy Christmas to you all. I hope you enjoy reading this book as much as I enjoyed writing it!

*The whistle blew, ripping the sacred solitude to rags and tatters. Then came the mind-numbing roar and thunder of the rushing wheels on iron track as the train wound its way through disheveled yards and out onto the great Salt Flats. The thousand-mile adventure had begun.*

# The Great Christmas
# Train Ride

*I*t was a Friday night, December 23, 1968, two days before Christmas. David sat alone at a long vacant dinner table, unable to face another recycled "breaded surprise" served in classic culinary style of the Cannon Center Cafeteria, where gravy was considered a beverage. Frankly, it looked a whole lot like the Goulash Crumb Special served just the night before.

"Even if they smothered this in chocolate," he muttered to no one in particular, "it would still be difficult to get it down."

He used his fork to idly push it from one side of the plate to the other, staring mindlessly out the window. An eerie gray quiet shrouded the world outside with all its inhabitants gripped in dirty gray ice. As dusk settled in, he could almost see another layer of ice forming over the month-long freeze, forcing the pitifully grotesque and disfigured plants ever deeper into hibernation just like all the rest of the world in this ghost town of a college campus.

"A Christmas to remember," he mused, feeling rather sorry for himself. "The perfect finale to my first semester in freshman purgatory. My home away from home, a world away from the California sunshine and my California girl."

The few meager presents he sent home for Christmas had taken a toll on his finances. After carefully combing through every nook and cranny in his dorm room, five dollars and twenty-eight cents was all that remained. He had converted it into quarters, and now absentmindedly weighed and measured their worth carefully in his pocket.

"To many, these twenty-one quarters and three cents might seem a paltry sum," he muttered to no one in particular, "but to me it's the fortune I need to make that long-awaited call home to Annie on Christmas day. That gluttonous pay phone gobbles up a quarter a minute, but it'll be worth it for those twenty-one precious minutes of her voice on the other end."

David looked down at the letter folded beside his plate, unfolded it, and—still brooding—read it once again. Since receiving the letter from Annie earlier that day, he had read it twice before dinner through the blurry haze of his eyes suffering from too much chlorine in the pool during water polo practice, preparation for the tournament scheduled just after the Christmas holidays over finals week.

To be fair, Annie had made a valiant effort to keep her spirits up for him, to appear cheerful while spending her own Christmas home alone. She was like that. But it was her letter's last line that pushed him over the edge: "If I had just one wish for this Christmas, David, I'd wish I could spend Christmas with you." That motivational wish stirred a longing in David that left him no alternative but to devise an uncommonly impulsive, but ingeniously brilliant plan that night, just two days before Christmas.

Suddenly, inspiration bounded into his very soul. He whirled from the window and began collecting his things in a rush to get out of the cafeteria. With a brilliant sparkle in his eye, he shouted, "Who says I have to be a pathetic loser over my Christmas vacation!" His loud voice startled to life the normally dispirited scattering of students in the almost empty cafeteria. "There is more to life than watching other people live it," he blurted out. Quickly, he wrapped the scrumptious "Breaded Surprise" in a bit of cellophane, stuffed it into the pocket of his old brown coat, then turned and hastily left the cafeteria.

Right then and there, he vowed to set aside all prudence and reason until after Christmas. David walked quickly out of the cafeteria, muttering quietly to himself, "It's all so simple really, and perfectly clear now. I have to go home for Christmas." He paused a half beat, then continued muttering into the night air, "I'll just hop a freight train home."

David rummaged through his dorm room collecting what he needed for the trip. He pulled on his old brown hat and grabbed the warmest thrift store hand-me-downs he could find from his closet, none of which would ever be found in the closet of any self-respecting, well-dressed man on campus.

"And of course, I can't forget my wetsuit because 'baby, it's cold out there.'" He would soon learn wearing a full wetsuit on a freight train in the dead of winter made it quite a production to take those essential visits to "The Necessary."

With a little trepidation in his heart, he swallowed his pride and called his good friend Georgie, asking her for a late night ride in her old jalopy to the freight train yards in the industrial wasteland of Salt Lake City's west side. It must have been the spirit of Christmas, for she agreed to brave the late night cold, snow, and black ice for the hour-and-a-half drive in Old Lizzy. Lizzy had no lights, wipers, or window cranks, leaving her windows permanently half open. She was tattooed in decals from bumper to bumper, with a bodaciously cool Jack O'Neil Surf sticker prominently placed in her rear window, courtesy of David.

It took Georgie's feminine touch just to coax her fickle Lizzy into doing her duty, but once Georgie got her started, no mortal man could stop that engine from running, certainly not just by turning off the key. And thankfully, Georgie was a magician with that emergency brake. Good thing, because it was the only way to stop the capricious Lizzy when the light turned red.

"Tell me again just why you're hopping the Union Pacific Freight Train to Sacramento in the middle of the night?" Georgie asked as they lumbered toward Salt Lake City on a hope and a prayer with fingers crossed.

"I'm taking my five dollars and twenty-eight cents and heading home for Christmas. I'm gonna surprise Annie with the best Christmas present ever—me!"

It was just after midnight when Georgie pulled up to the derelict, rusty old gate laid open to expose a foreboding freight yard locked in a frozen world. With obvious concern in her voice, she solemnly wished him a "Merry Christmas," and then offered a worried, "Please, please be safe."

He looked around tentatively, stepped out of the car, pulled on his backpack, and with a restless uneasiness, turned back to Georgie to offer an anxious goodbye.

She managed to return an encouraging smile. "Buck up, Private." Then she blew him a sympathetic kiss to seal it.

His confidence clearly rattled, he pulled himself together and smiled back, trying not to expose his apprehensiveness.

She pushed open the door, walked over, and gave him a big concerned hug, "If it doesn't work out, call me. I'll come pick you up." Then she was gone.

He walked through the gate into a rambling train yard, cluttered with shadowy images, drenched in a disquieting haze of smoky soot and grime; the entire yard was illuminated by only a single light in the distance. Freight trains sprawled out in every direction—meandering helter-skelter, heading this way and that. There was no telling which one was going where. As he approached the distant light flickering through a dirty, cracked window, he could see inside the railroad security guards bundled up in front of a fire.

As snow began to fall, the wind whipped at his face forcing him deeper into the collar of his coat. "Well, now what do I do?" he said aloud, recognizing the difficult task ahead. From train to train he trudged, through the dispiriting snowfall. The few empty cars he saw were rusty and filthy.

Discouraged and frustrated, he abruptly turned back on his heel, only to find himself confronted face to face with a railroad security guard. Both stood staring at each other. There was no avenue of escape. He was busted!

"What are you doing here, boy?" the guard asked irritably.

David slid his hand over the back of his neck and stumbled through an explanation. "I'm sorry, sir, but I really need to go home to Sacramento for Christmas, and I have no money."

Maybe it was the spirit of Christmas, but the security guard's face seemed to relax, and the irritated resistance seemed to soften.

"Sacramento, huh?" He paused, taking the measure of David. "Well, that would be UP 321, leaving at 2:00 a.m. Here, you might as well follow me. Let's at least find you a refrigerator car that's out of service. It'll be the warmest and cleanest."

"Thank you, sir! Thank you so much. I really appreciate this," David said, breathing a sigh of relief as he humbly fell in behind the guard and followed his lead.

The guard led David down the tracks to a large enclosed car. He slid open the door. David stepped up to the bed of the open car, turned, and smiled at the guard in appreciation for his kindness, then climbed in. Heavy snow was falling now. Before he could turn back, the security guard was gone without a word. But moments later, the guard returned with his arms full of cardboard.

"Here, a little protection against the cold," he said. "Merry Christmas, son. I hope you make it."

"Thank you, sir. Merry Christmas to you. You've been very kind!"

And with a tip of his cap the guard was gone.

Using the cardboard, David tried to make himself as warm and as comfortable as he could. He then pulled out the cold Breaded Surprise, which had suffered a bit from time spent in his pocket. Sitting against the inside wall of the refrigerator car, covered in cardboard, he ate his dinner while staring out into the dark cold, cloud-covered night.

The whistle blew promptly at 2:00 a.m., "ripping the sacred solitude to rags and tatters."[1] The train began to move, winding its way through the disheveled yards and out onto the Great Salt Flats. His thousand-mile adventure had begun. He had every hope of being home for Christmas.

With the clickety-clack rumble of steel wheels rolling on iron tracks they left the Salt Lake Valley behind. He sat wrapped in cardboard, staring out of the open door as the train slowly chugged through unrecognizable terrain. The falling snow stopped, the skies cleared, and a full moon shined bright on the crisp new fallen snow blanketing the treeless rolling plains. There was no evidence of man in sight except the two solitary rails of track that lay in front of them. "The simple beauty of nature," David thought, then remembering a quote he learned in freshman English. "Life is not about the number of breaths you take really—it's about the moments that take your breath away!"[2]

They seemed far from the maddening crowd as the train passed over Promontory Point. He leaned back, a thoughtful smile spread across his face, and in a moment he was lost in his thoughts as what seemed a seldom seen world slid by. A century ago, there had been great commotion at this very spot.

"My own great-grandfather probably laid the very track I'm passing over," he whispered into the night.

With his new wife, also named Annie, Thomas Wright immigrated to America—first by freighter, then by wagon train across the American Continent to work for the Union Pacific Railroad. For sixteen hours a day, seven days a week, he labored shoulder to shoulder with other immigrants from all around the world; some days laying up to ten miles of track and living his nights among "Hell on Wheels."

David mused, "My great-great-grandfather was right here at this very spot, together with risk-taking entrepreneurs and other adventurous pioneers, they built this Trans-Continental rail line, probably the greatest engineering marvel of the nineteenth century; the wonder of nature meeting the imagination of man; the linking of America from east to west; from sea to shining sea."

Abraham Lincoln well knew that final golden spike driven into the ground at Promontory Point on May 10, 1869, would secure the Union and it would secure the destiny of America!

The incessant mind-numbing roar and thunder of rushing wheels on iron track made it virtually impossible to sleep as the train rumbled along all through the long night. Visions of cuddling up with Annie in front of an open fire danced in his head. Still, it took thousands of jumping jacks and hundreds of push-ups to shed the cold.

Just as dawn peeked over the horizon, the train stopped. Slowly, he ventured out into the sacred solitude of early morning. The pale cold sunlight bathed the newly fallen snow in a soft radiance.

Well off in the distance he could see a solitary country road lined in leafless cottonwoods; next to it, a lonely gas station. Summoning his courage, he jumped down from the open doorway and ran the distance to the gas station.

"Excuse me, sir, where are we? Are we in Nevada?" David asked the station attendant while casting a glance toward the train down on the flat below them.

"No, son, you're in Utah still," the station attendant informed him. "Nevada's still a piece down the road."

David squinted his eyes, looking warily toward the refrigerator car in the distance. He continued to stare in that direction as he pulled the quarters out of his pocket and bought everything he could from the candy machine.

"Did it move?" he questioned himself, intensely aware that any forward movement could spell trouble for him at this great distance. Then, the whistle blew its unwelcome warning. His eyes sharpened their focus intently on the faraway train. It was indeed on the move. He stuffed the candy into his pocket and ran hell-bent in chase after the train as it slowly pulled away down the track, picking up speed as it went.

"Oh my gosh!" He panicked and began to run after it. He ran down the hill, crossed the flat, then ran along the gravel berm paralleling the train. He ran as fast as he could to catch up to the refrigerator car, but the train was slowly picking up speed. The cold air cut his lungs and his thighs burned hot as he reached the open door of the refrigerator car. Then the train lunged forward faster than he could run. It seemed to be moving twice as fast now as it did when he was riding in it. Was he just too tired to catch up? Finally he was there in front of the open door. He threw his arms and elbows up onto the floor of the car, legs swinging between the spinning wheels. After struggling and kicking for what seemed an eternity, he finally pulled himself aboard.

Panting desperately to catch his breath, sucking in all the air his lungs would hold, he lay on the floor of the open car, facing the ceiling. After some moments when he knew he wasn't going to hyperventilate to death, he threw his arms back over his head and began to laugh. "I can't believe I just did that. What am I doing out here in the middle of nowhere?"

All the day long the train lumbered along, seldom passing any sign of life to let him know just where they might be or where they were going next, except heading west into the great expanse of a wind-whipped frozen Nevada wasteland east of Hells Kitchen Canyon. Dusk came and night fell. Once again the train stopped.

It had been a night and a day of traveling without sleep. Far off in the distance he could see the lights of a town. After two hours of jumping jacks to keep warm in the cold night air, he decided those lights had to be Reno, and the best thing to do was hike out in that direction. So with single-minded focus, off he went into the cloud-covered darkness, heading straight toward the light.

Unconcerned for what calamities might lie in his path, David moved quickly across the open fields separating him from the town. He didn't notice the ground shift from coarse, uneven terrain to smooth slick ice until it was too late. A crack splintered under his feet, dumping him waist deep into the muddy water of an iced-over irrigation ditch. He was soaked to the bone, his boots stuck into the muddy bottom. With great effort he broke himself free of the mud, slogged his way out of the ditch, and trudged the remaining three miles into town. He was colder than a brass toilet seat on the Yukon.

It wasn't Reno after all, but Winnemucca, Nevada. Broken down cowboy bars, derelict casinos, and beat-up old pick-ups lined Main Street. The flicker of neon lights punctuated the smoky haze of exhaust fumes drifting through the cold night air.

Hungry, muddy, and near frozen, David wandered though the dilapidated, smoke-filled gambling lounges, trying to parlay the few remaining quarters left rattling around in his pocket into something to eat and a ride further west. Reno was still four hundred miles away.

His efforts failed pitifully. So he put out his thumb and tried hitch-hiking down Main Street, where it was painfully clear women in Winnemucca would never be equal to men until they could walk down the street with a bald head and a beer gut, and still think they're sexy.

Cold, with no more money, the only response from the local Winnemuccans was the cowboy stink-eye. Just when he thought things couldn't get any worse, the local sheriff pulled up.

"There ain't no hitchhiking here in Winnemucca," he advised. "Not a word now, son. You're looking like an idiot out here. I'd advise you not to open your mouth and remove any doubt about it." With that, he gave David a lift to the outskirts of town. "Don't come back now, you hear?"

It was after midnight and snowing, on Christmas Eve, and no one was going his way. Locked in a nightmare from which he was trying desperately to awake, he fell deep into conversation with himself. "How cold can it get here before I have to walk back into town and spend Christmas Eve in a jail cell?" he said to himself while rummaging through his backpack to find his matches and what nonessential study sheets brought along to prepare for after Christmas finals. Finally he found what he needed but the cold night air had left the matches damp.

The first several matches failed to light the crumpled study sheets and the few meager sticks of damp brush he could find. He could hardly feel his near frozen fingers, but managed to strike another match, again without success. "My gosh, I feel more like one of God's frozen children," he complained to himself. "It seems a wonder to me, that while a careless match can start a raging forest fire, I have used nearly a whole box of matches and can't even start a simple campfire on the side of the road." He took out another damp match. "Money may not buy me happiness, but it sure would make this miserable night a whole lot easier to live through."

When he had just about given up all hope and was ready to walk back into town and surrender himself to the jailer, a little old man pulled up in a battered Datsun pickup.

"Going my way, son? This ain't no place to spend your Christmas."

Without a moment's hesitation, David jumped into the cab of that beat-up little pickup before the old man could change his mind.

"The name's Jo Bonnie," he offered, welcoming David with a bag of chips. "Slide your hands under the dash, in front of the heater. It's warm as a chipmunk's den in winter."

"Jo Bonnie—that's Portuguese isn't it?" David responded, trying to make a little conversation. "I'm Portuguese as well."

"A Portagee, huh. There's only two kinds of people in this here world— those who's Portagee, and those who's a wishing they was a Portagee," Jo Bonnie informed him. "You know it was the Portagee who discovered America and just about everything else in this here world for that matter."

With all the potato chips David could eat and sodas he could drink, he wasn't about to quibble over a mildly distorted history lesson. Besides, Jo Bonnie was a compassionate old soul who had an oversized heart with a friendly and contagious smile. For six straight hours David listened to this little old fellow talk a mile a minute. With homespun intelligence, sharing one of mankind's greatest gifts—humor—old Jo Bonnie told stories of riding the rails during the Great Depression.

Jo Bonnie dropped David off right at the Reno freight yard with a bit of invaluable advice: "Slip into the empty engine in tow, see; it's got heat, a john, and plenty a water. Every train has a couple spare engines in tow. But don't you'ins get youself caught heading up over the Sierra's—they'll skin you alive, then boot you out in the snow."

Jo Bonnie smiled mischievously as he sent David on his way. "Merry Christmas, and a good luck to you, son."

Sure enough, David found a train heading west over the mighty Sierra Nevada Mountains with three engines in tow. It was clear to him his luck had changed. Old Jo Bonnie had it right all along; the cab was equipped with a perfectly fine heater, a five-gallon water dispenser, restroom, and the most comfortable chair ever built by man. He settled in for the ride home in style.

Two hours into the ride the train stopped at the Summit Base Camp for last minute supplies before heading over Donner Pass. Just to be safe David slipped out of the cab and climbed into the open coal car behind— just until the coast was clear and the train started up again. Easy-peasy!

He looked on in disbelief as an off-duty railroad engineer climbed into that engine cab clearly settling in for the remainder of the trip into Sacramento. What could he do, but make the best of the rest of the train ride over the summit in the rusty old open coal car; no easy task at 7,000 feet in the dead of winter. He tucked himself in as best he could. The ice encrusted, rusted-out bottom of the open car had been designed to carry coal, not lonely hitchhikers.

The clickety-clack of steel wheels rolling over disjointed track had echoed through these treacherously beautiful Sierra-Nevada Mountains for more than a hundred years since this stretch of track had been completed, costing hundreds of lives—mostly Chinese immigrants.

Well, at least the sun was out which was some consolation. Until it wasn't, and the snow started falling again. This was a new kind of cold. It seeped deep into his bones. Not even the wetsuit seemed to make a difference. He curled up in the corner to preserve what little warmth his body could generate. As they wound their way through Donner Pass, David's mind drifted off into hypothermic delusions.

It seemed quite reasonable now to imagine some Union Pacific railroad man finding his body permanently frozen to the iron bulkhead of this rusty old coal bucket before the day was done. He tried to offer a little prayer, "Lord, I am so sorry for putting You in this position. I suppose imperfect people like me are often all You have to work with. It must be terribly frustrating, but I'm guessing You've learned a thing or two about dealing with folks like me. Please, I need your help."

Sometimes we forget that the Lord never leaves us entirely alone. He watches over us especially in our most challenging moments when we often think we really don't deserve it. Sometimes He sends us angels in our dark and dreary places. Though we may imagine them as immortal, sometimes they're mortal angels. In his delusional state, David heard a voice, a question drifting down from above seemingly out of the heavens: "Would you like to join me in the engine cab, son?"

With a kind word and a strong arm, the off-duty railroad engineer helped David into the comforting warmth of the cab. He sat him down on that most comfortable seat. "I'm Mike," he said as he offered David a hot cup of hot chocolate. That first sip was one of the most beautiful experiences in David's life. And after a time, his hands began to thaw. Heaven never seems closer than when we are on the receiving end of kindness manifested through one of God's emissaries in our midst.

When they finally arrived in Sacramento, dusk was falling on Christmas Eve. Mike offered David a ride across town. Of course that meant driving in the opposite direction of his home and family in Christmas Eve traffic. But without comment, he delivered David to his final destination.

"I couldn't have made it without you, Mike! Really—I'm serious, thank you!"

"You're welcome. If we haven't a little charity in our heart, well, we have the worst kind of heart trouble, don't we! Merry Christmas, David!"

David walked through the apartment complex he knew so well. It was as if he hadn't even been gone these past few months. Suddenly anxious, the palms of his hands began to sweat. He took a deep breath to regain his composure. Then a smile began to spread across his face as he imagined the shock and surprise on Annie's face when she saw him standing at the door.

He knocked, took a step back and another deep breath, and just waited for what seemed a very long time, until finally the door opened. For some reason he hadn't even considered Marsha, Annie's roommate answering the door, but there she stood immovable, staring at him without a word. Her stunned eyes fixed on him. The intoxication of reaching his goal after the two-day journey suddenly gave way to an uncomfortable awareness of just how he must look—like Pig Pen coming to pick up Lucy. Self-consciously, he fumbled to tuck a cloud of unruly hair back under his shabby old brown hat, then slid his grimy hands into his back pockets.

There was an expression on Marsha he could not read. It wasn't disapproval, not horror, nor any of the sentiments he would have expected. She simply stared at him fixedly with that peculiar expression on her face.

"David, you're supposed to be in Utah!"

"Well, I'm here. I came home to be with Annie for Christmas. It's kind of a surprise," he awkwardly explained, looking back at her with an unmistakable question in his eyes.

"But you're here—not in Utah," she repeated, ignoring his question and struggling to master the obvious.

"So, Marsha, is she here?"

"It's kind of a surprise, all right," Marsha finally responded as the astonishment of his presence finally began to register. "You probably should have called—it's always better to know which way the tornado is coming from than to be surprised."

Clearly Marsha was searching for just what she should say next. "Well, you better come in. Sit down and try to make yourself comfortable. I'll make you a cup of something warm to drink."

He, of course, did as he was told, sitting on the edge of the couch in anticipation. Marsha departed into the kitchen, returning shortly with mugs of hot cinnamon tea for both of them.

"David, Annie's not here because she flew to Utah to surprise you for Christmas. After giving up looking for you, she has been trying all day to get a flight home, but it's Christmas Eve. There are no flights to be had. I am so very, very sorry. Annie won't be home for Christmas."

He sat silently stirring his tea and trying to make sense of this stunning revelation. He felt rather foolish and profoundly disappointed, yet intrigued by Annie's willingness to fly all the way to Utah just to see him. The implications didn't go unnoticed.

"Really, she went all the way to Utah—just to see me?"

"Yes, and you know how she can't stand the cold. When it drops below 75 degrees, she puts on her mufflers." Marsha laughed, trying to lighten the mood. "And they got weather in Utah, don't they?"

"She must really like me?"

"Definitely!" Marsha smiled. "I'm so sorry your Love Santa got caught in the chimney, David."

Marsha was tender and kind, but despite her valiant effort to cheer him up, he was left with little to say. After almost three days without sleep, he suddenly felt tired . . . so very, very tired.

He had braved cold nights, long days, snow, and ice, with little to eat on $5.28. He had traveled more than a thousand miles over salt flats, high desert plains frozen like a popsicle, and two mountain ranges, only to find her, the reason for all of it gone to Utah!

David tumbled back into the couch, put his hands behind the back of his head, and settled in as a thoughtful grin eased into a capitulating smile. "I suppose then, this is the point where I should surrender to my fate?"

Marsha looked at him quizzically, and then asked the inevitable question, "So how was your trip? You look a little worse for wear."

And with a smile he told her the whole of it.

Marsha took it all in. "Pretty amusing. Frankly, you can't accuse either of you of keeping one foot on the shoreline. You've both jumped into the deep end without a life preserver. Well over your head, I'd say. You know you're both fully insane, don't you?" Martha smiled. "Both of you making the same irrational, impulsive decisions—really, David, hopping a freight train for a two-day ride over the Rockies and Sierra Nevada Mountains in the dead of winter just to see your girlfriend?"

With a twinkle in her eye and a sly mischievous smile easing across her face, Marsha observed, "Very unusual behavior; downright reckless some might say!"

She paused to form a question. "You know what they call it when uncharacteristically impetuous acts like these come together with unexplained, irrational, obsessive-compulsive behavior . . . don't you?"

"Yeah, the Bermuda Triangle," he answered with a grin.

Suddenly in unison, they turned their gaze toward the front door. The lock turned, the door slowly swung open. And there she stood, tired and forlorn, his beautiful California girl.

He stood awkwardly to greet her as she entered the room. She hadn't yet noticed him standing there in his tattered and disheveled clothes covered in coal dust, crusted mud, and rusty stains. His filthy, worn-out muddy clodhopper shoes and grungy wetsuit collar still showing. He pulled off his rumpled brown hat and ran a grimy hand through his matted hair in a pathetic attempt to make a difference.

She looked up in surprise just in time to see his engaging smile spreading wide across an exhausted, coal dust-smudged face.

"Hello, gorgeous," he said.

And all she saw were his warm, inviting eyes and wide, infectious smile. In reflection, her tired countenance gave way to a bright and ardent spirit with a sparkle in her crystal-clear green eyes; a warm glow lit up her face like a bright light in the night.

"Oh my," she said, a little lost for words. "Merry Christmas. You won't believe the story I have to tell about my last twenty-four hours sitting in the airport."

It was a memory to be cherished as Marsha took it all in with a smile, trying to wipe away the tears filling her own eyes.

Nobody really knows how great love happens. One day you're going about your business enjoying life, and the next you can't imagine life without her.

＊ ＊ ＊

For all of us fellow travelers through life, this earthly adventure is a lot like riding the rails—expect long delays, setbacks, smoke, dust, cinders, uncomfortable weather, and far too frequent jolts that keep our attention from wandering, interspersed with occasional beautiful vistas and thrilling bursts of exciting speed while our legs dangle out the doorway of the open car. The trick is to thank the Lord for the ride. We are especially aware during the Christmas season, when the Spirit of Christmas abounds and we are poignantly reminded that we are not placed on this earth to walk alone.

The spirit of Christmas, of course is the spirit of Christ can be found in every man where there is charity, love, and gratitude for his fellow travelers through life. Without it, well then, we are missing out on the best of what life has to offer, aren't we?

True charity requires action one to another, often in very simple ways. It's the young woman who sacrifices her time to drive a friend in her beat-up old jalopy to his destination in the middle of the night. It's the railroad security guard who steps out into the cold and puts aside company policy to help a poor boy into the right railroad car, then sends him on his way as best he can. It's the old gentleman who goes out of his way to offer the wayfarer a ride for a few miles in the warmth of his battered pickup truck. It's the kind thoughtfulness of the off-duty railroad engineer, who shares his small but warm space with the dirty hobo on a frigid mountaintop. It is the roommate, who in her concern for a broken spirit, sweetly shares her time and encouraging kindness to soften disappointment.

But the wisest gift of them all is a willingness to sacrifice of oneself for the love of another. This is Christ's great atoning example to us all: "Love one another; as I have loved you,"[3] with self-sacrifice and lovingkindness. There is no room for pride, prejudice, vanity, or fear in your heart when it is full of love, one for another. It is love that can alter human lives. It is love, the catalyst to change human nature. It is love, "the balm that brings healing to the soul."[4] And finally, it is the acknowledgment of these gifts and the offering of gratitude for them that embodies the best of the Christmas spirit.

May we have the spirit of Christmas, the Spirit of Christ, not for one fleeting day each year but every moment of every day.

God bless us, everyone, and a Merry Christmas to you all!

*Five-year-old Kirra skating the bowl in her ballet tutu!*

# Skate Rising

alli Kelsay—the mother of "three amazing little girls and one incredible, very rambunctious little boy," as she describes them—is the type of mother who if she saw only four pieces of pie left for dessert would announce to her family she never really cared much for pie anyway.

According to Calli, "My children always come first, except for maybe my husband, Matt, who is the most handsome and interesting man alive."

Both Calli and Matt work hard to elicit kindness and foster compassionate service in their home, and their children are frequently rewarded one-on-one time with the parent of their choice for surprise adventures as compensation for accumulated random acts of kindness to their siblings, friends, or neighbors. All are encouraged to follow the Kelsay family golden rule: to proceed with confidence, compassion, and perseverance in everything you do and never forget you are always on the Lord's errand to lift the lives of those around you. It is just a part of who they are as a family.

It is this underlying current of values running deep in the Kelsay home that spawned a revolutionary idea, an idea propelled by Calli's enthusiasm and resolve to make a difference. It is an idea that has changed the lives of their family, their community, and the world well beyond. It is an idea that has empowered girls to embrace confidence, compassion, and perseverance in everything they do.

※ ※ ※

One summer, not so long ago, Calli and Matt spent almost every Saturday morning surfing with their three girls on the beaches of Encinitas, California, where Calli is sure some archeologist, a thousand years from now, will find her bones buried in the sand. Calli's father (a very accomplished surfer himself), other family members, and heaps of friends frequently joined in on their Saturday morning fun at the beach. It was a time when the family could bond with one another, strengthen friendships, and learn of life's blessings along the way.

Matt would push his daughters Aubrey and Kirra, ages seven and five, into the shore break waves while Grandpa would ride in on a wave with two-year-old Juliet perched on his lap. Chase, their little boy, had not yet joined the family and frankly was not even on the radar. It was a great summer followed by a warm fall.

All grew closer together as family and friends, but with winter came the cold and an end to regular Saturday-morning beach excursions. So the girls took up skateboarding—not a conventional outlet most moms have in mind for their girls, and Matt wasn't particularly sure about it either. But Calli has an uncanny ability to integrate the preeminent values of the family's golden rule into her children's activities, even when pursuing the most seemingly unrelated endeavors. She supported and encouraged her girls in their skating, but with the Calli twist—invite any girls that show an interest into the fold and incorporate into their skating the family's golden rule.

Calli even set up monthly outings at the renowned Encinitas Skate Park with her girls, their friends, and any girl who might like to participate. But, of course, there was a catch: to include a life lesson of service with each monthly skateboard outing.

They called themselves "Skate Rising, a community of girls rising by lifting other girls to greater heights and serving one another and their community with unconditional love." They would learn to gain the confidence to skate with the boys, to search out community needs and opportunities, and make a difference in other peoples' lives wherever they found an opportunity.

It was difficult at first, the mostly teenage boys at the skate park were sometimes frightening and not particularly encouraging. Especially when five-year-old Kirra showed up in her ballet tutu (which now, at age eight, has become her trademark). But Calli was there to encourage her girls and deliver her own signature knock-out punch to the boys. She disabled them with kindness and understanding, which has a way of endearing even the most recalcitrant, rebellious teenage boy. For lovingkindness is a language that all understand. It is the balm that soothes hurt feelings and the catalyst of change.

Calli and her girls are a joy to be around, so everyone one wanted to be around them, and it wasn't long before fourteen- to nineteen-year-old skater dudes were down on bended knee helping the little girls learn to skate. And when the girls fell, the boys helped them get back up to try again, for they had learned that success isn't the absence of failure, but instead it is going from one failure to another without the loss of enthusiasm.[1]

In time, the girls were skating the bowl, even some in their tutus. The older, wiser, more-experienced, and supposedly hardened teenage boys were on the sidelines smiling and clacking their boards in support and encouragement. As Calli's golden rule slowly softened the hearts of even the most hard-core skater, these skating events at the park became an incubator for mutual encouragement and support.

Calli had a vision that Skate Rising could be more than just a small group of girls skating and trying to do a few good deeds in their neighborhood. She thought their golden rule, the cornerstone of Skate Rising, could change lives for the better and even change the world around them. But as always, many were skeptical. "It's a dangerous sport that girls shouldn't be involved with," some suggested. "There is an antisocial element in the skating community that is not good for children. And besides, the girls will lose interest in service projects. After all, how many opportunities are there for these young girls to be kind and helpful and to serve your neighbors anyway?"

But Calli, her supporters, and the girls were resolute. In just over a year of monthly outings, Skate Rising grew exponentially from a few neighborhood girls to often over seventy-five girls participating in a single monthly event at the Encinitas Skate Park, with some monthly events drawing over one hundred girls, serving needs all over San Diego County and beyond to folks from all walks of life. Skate Rising has provided hundreds of survival kits filled with essentials to immigrant refugee families; addressed the needs of underprivileged youth and fatherless or orphaned children; helped out the Rady Children's Hospital; provided backpacks for underprivileged and homeless children and victims of domestic violence, food for the poor, and gifts for children of battered wives; and completed many other similar projects. They were a force to be reckoned with and realizing the vision of Skate Rising: it seemed there was nothing they couldn't do.

\* \* \*

Lillian thought it quite possible she was Skate Rising's biggest fan and most enthusiastic member of the team. She had been introduced by a friend from school to Calli, the girls, and skating at the Holiday Skate during the previous Christmas. Lillian had to admit, "On that first day, I was undoubtedly the most nervous skater ever to walk through the gates of the Encinitas Skate Park, with my borrowed skateboard and absolutely horrid helmet. It was orange, ugly, and totally clashed with my outfit."

Notwithstanding, she was hooked from the start. "I had brought a present, as requested, to be given to one of the little girls at the Battered Women's Shelter," Lillian would later tell her mom, Elizabeth. "That day was totally awesome!"

"It was by far the coolest thing I had ever done in my whole entire life. The look on this little girl's face from the shelter when I gave her the gift just about melted my heart, Mom. She was just so darn cute, all the little children there were," Lillian told Elizabeth after. "It was just so touching to see that little girl smiling and laughing so."

That was a year ago, before Lillian became a regular member of this community of girls rising by lifting other girls to greater heights. "Of course, I was only nine back then," she recalled later. "Now I'm a whole year older and far more experienced, but still the Holiday Skate was by far my favorite."

Lillian's second-best day came when her mom gave her a "Stevie-G" skateboard. Lillian's eyes shined brightly when she first held it in her arms. This was her most prized possession in all the world. So much so she took it to school that first day "so all the other kids could look on it in envy."

Lillian never missed a single skating event after the Holiday Skate the previous Christmas and participated in every service project as well, "which I really always liked the best," she said.

Of course, that was until October when Lillian started having dizzy spells. By then, she had become a pretty good skateboarder and could skate the bowl as well as any of the other girls. She seldom fell anymore. But on that day, she had fallen off her skateboard when a dizzy spell hit. "I was riding the bowl at the skate park. The fall didn't really hurt that much, but I was still dizzy after." She couldn't seem to get rid of the dizziness, so her mom took her to the doctor.

"The doctors and nurses were so nice," she later said to her mom, "but it was really tiring with all the tests, tests, and more tests."

For a week they poked, prodded, and took tests, then the doctor brought her into his office. Her mom was already with him when Lillian came through the door to the doctors office and she could tell her mom had been crying from her red, moist eyes.

The doctor looked at Lillian very seriously, "I'm sorry to tell you Lillian, but you have cancer in your brain. Do you know what cancer is, Lillian?"

"No, not really," she answered, but by the look on the faces of the doctor and her mom, Lillian knew it wasn't good.

Worry is the price of a mother's love for her child and part of the job sometimes requires a mother to do things that seem too much to ask of anyone. "When you're told your beautiful little girl is critically ill with cancer, your whole world goes numb. Cancer dominates your thoughts, it is debilitating," Elizabeth would later say. "You don't remember coming home from the doctor's office. Just finding a matching pair of shoes and socks each day becomes a challenge. Shopping for dinner, doing the laundry, cleaning the house, going to doctors, the endless tests, all become horrendous undertakings, and then comes the treatment which sometimes seems worse than the cancer."

Over the next two months, all the doctors, tests, treatment, and physical therapy in Lillian's life became very taxing on this little girl and her family, but even more perplexing for the ten-year-old was how things would never be the same. She looked to her mom for answers to questions her mom was still grappling to understand herself. "What does terminal mean, Mom?" Lillian asked. But Elizabeth wasn't sure how to answer her sweet little girl.

Lillian had constant double vision now, causing her to lose control of her balance and her muscles. She spent her days in a wheelchair. But she was tough and seldom lost her composure, for her toughness was in her soul and spirit of life, not in her muscles that seemed to be functioning properly less and less each day.

Of course, the effects of the cancer on her brain and her body were scary and she was afraid. But sometimes you have no choice but to go through things and not around them. Lillian may not have been able to redirect the wind that brought this cancer into her life, but she was determined to adjust her sails to face the stiff winds of challenge head-on, to live out the remainder of her life on her own terms. She had learned that much from Skate Rising, to face life with courage and perseverance.

"Perseverance," Calli would say, "is what you do with your life when you're told it can't be done, you just do it anyway. The scientist, who after 487 failed experiments, discovers penicillin. Thomas Edison who tried the 10,000 ways that didn't work, before he found the one that did. George Washington, leading a rag-tag militia without shoes, in the freezing dead of winter, doesn't have a prayer of defeating the greatest army the world had ever known, then does it anyway. Sometimes those who are telling us why it can't be done, are interrupted by those just doing it. The secret is simple really: when you fall down, you just get back up and try again. Simple, but not so easily done, especially when the world around you says, 'you can't do it!'"

Says Calli, "The world is full of those who have been told it's not possible, then do it anyway. Just ask Seabiscuit!"

Frankly, Lillian had just about enough of all the doctors, tests, treatments, prodding and poking. She just wanted to be with her friends and feel of their spirit, their kindness, and their support to help her with the courage and perseverance to stay the course to the very end.

With Christmas season upon them Lillian wanted a break from the protocol of tests and treatment. After talking to her mom, she called Calli. "I'm sorry I've missed the past couple of months, but I've been sick," Lillian apologized, then sweetly asked, "But do you think I might attend the Holiday Skate coming up? I won't be able to actually skate, but I would sure like to see all the girls and participate in the service project."

"Sure Lillian, we would love to have you come and participate any way you can," Calli said. "I have asked all the girls to bring either their favorite gift to give away, or maybe one of their favorite things they have at home. It's up to you what to give. You think about it Lillian—does that sound okay to you?"

There are only two ways one can live life. Either as a cynic seeing only the negative and dwelling on the hardship of life, or like Lilian, an optimist seeing life for what it really is, a miracle. Lillian began to prepare with her mom to go to the Holiday Skate, to see all her friends again and share something with someone else in need.

She knew now she would have some hard days ahead of her, but was determined to fight through them. "Who knows, maybe my best days are still in front of me," she told her mom, who smiled in total and complete admiration for her little girl.

She thought long and hard about what she might give to a young girl. She wanted it to be something special, to be something she held dear, something precious to her, something that would bring a bright smile to a little girl in need.

There was really only one possession Lillian had that met the criteria, only one thing that important to her: her "Stevie-G" skateboard. With her eyes shining brightly, she gazed fondly at her board mounted in the preeminent spot on her bedroom wall. She reached up and pulled it down, held it in her hands, felt its weight, and judged its worth. It was her prized possession and would make a wonderful gift. But with the thought of giving it up for good, the color left her face and moisture came to her eyes. "No, I'm not going to feel sorry for myself," Lillian said, taking a deep breath and quickly putting the skateboard out of sight in the closet. Her decision had been made, firm and fast. It was final: "This is what I will give some deserving little girl."

❋ ❋ ❋

The day came, her mom wheeled Lillian up to the table that had been set up just outside the Encinitas Skate Park to collect all the gifts from the girls. She handed over her "Stevie-G" skateboard, wrapped in a bow, with a sweet little note sharing her thoughts to the future owner, the future receiver of her treasure.

There were gifts of every kind piled up on the table. It was the most amazing outpouring of love she had ever seen. "There are gonna be some very happy little girls, Mom," Lillian said, to which Elizabeth quietly responded from behind Lillian's wheelchair with a squeeze of Lillian's shoulders. She did not speak for fear of letting her emotions get the better of her.

Elizabeth pushed her daughter toward the gate into the skate park. Excited, Lillian turned around in her wheelchair to smile up at her mom. Elizabeth returned the contagious smile with a warm smile of her own, but it came with a tear, not too uncommon these days.

When Lillian and her mom passed through the gates into the Encinitas Skate Park, the entire park erupted in cheers and applause. They were all standing, clacking their skate boards, clapping their hands, and smiling. There were more than a hundred girls, their moms and dads, and other skaters too.

"What is this?" asked Lillian, her mind not yet arriving at a patent understanding of the crowd's reaction to her arrival. "What are they cheering for, Mom?"

Lillian turned to look back at her mom for an answer. But Elizabeth could not bring to voice an answer. Tears now cascading down her face, she could only caress Lillian's shoulders once more in response as love passed from mother to daughter without the necessity of the spoken word.

Lillian turned back and looked about the park in curious puzzlement, the balloons, the tents and all the people, many smiling, but with tears in their eyes. They all seemed to be looking at her. Finally, understanding seeped into Lillian's mind and heart. She was the one in need this time, and all had come to brighten her Christmas.

Blessed is the season which engaged Lillian's whole world in a clandestine conspiracy of love. It was her turn to cry. Indeed, sometimes it takes bad days to recognize the best of days in our lives when they come.

All the girls rushed Lillian with hugs and kisses and best Merry Christmas wishes. There were presents of every kind. Then Stevie-G appeared, her favorite pro-skater in all the world.

"What are you doing here?" Lillian asked in amazement. "How did you get here?"

"I came for you, Lillian. We all came for you!" He held in his hands a magnificent skateboard built in the shape of a heart. "I designed this just for you and had it painted with your favorite color of purple." He smiled. "Personalized just for you, Lillian." Then he took out a black permanent marker and signed it. In fact, before the day was done, Lillian's new board was covered in signatures from her favorite skaters—now her friends.

Her friends helped her to stand on her new board. Supported with their loving, steady hands, Lillian skated around the park. Everyone clapped, smiled, and clacked their boards as she passed them by. "This is the best day of my life!" she shouted above the noise, smiling as though she were without a care in the world.

When the moment had passed and quiet once again settled in, Calli knelt down to give Lillian a hug and a kiss. "You know, Lillian, cancer can take away a lot of things, mostly physical, the use of your arms and legs and things like that," said Calli. "But it cannot take away who you are, your beautiful kindness, your caring heart, or your sweet spirit." Lillian was smiling and wiping at her moist eyes as Calli continued. "Always remember you are not alone," Calli told her. "We have missed you so much, Lillian, and I want you to promise me you will always think of us as those who love you. Promise me you will call me or any of the girls whenever you feel down."

"Thank you, Calli. I promise."

✳ ✳ ✳

"Cancer is that awful word we all fear, but in that brief dark moment when I first heard, 'Your little girl has cancer,' windows were opened to my mind. There was a new understanding of the world we live in and of the people we share it with. The beauty of simple things I had not even noticed before were now illuminated in my heart," Elizabeth shared. "What Calli and the girls of Skate Rising did for my daughter in this very difficult time will never be forgotten by my family. It's not just the money raised to offset medical costs, the many presents, or the offerings, but it's the kindness, love, and compassion shown to my little girl when she so desperately needed it. It buoyed her spirit and brought a smile of thanksgiving to her lips. It was the sweetest smile I had seen in a very long time. Those moments were like diamonds to my little girl and to all of us in our family. They shifted my view of the world from a place of fear, to a place of endless love."

✳ ✳ ✳

It's not the amount of time God gives us that counts, but what we do with the time we are given that matters. We don't always get what we think we want, but as we step outside ourselves and serve one another in Christ, the Lord will give us what we need and all will be well in our search for happiness. It may not come today. It may not come tomorrow. It may not even come until after this life is over. But whether in this life or the next, it will come.

When we pass through the world, following the simple admonition of our Savior to love each other as ourselves, oftentimes lives are changed for the better. It is often by simple acts of kindness and tender mercies offered that the miracle of Christmas seeps into the hearts of those around us, sometimes making all the difference and transforming lives forever.

Calli knelt in prayer following the Christmas event for Lillian. "Every night, Father in Heaven, I kneel down to unload my problems on Your shoulders. I'm so sorry about that, but then I presume You're going to be up all night anyway, aren't You? I have a lot to learn, don't I? I suppose all of us do. I suppose that's why You give us these beautiful children like Lillian, children who break our hearts. I suppose it's to teach us a little of the suffering You have had to bear for us and remind us to express our gratitude for life experiences. Lillian is such a beautiful child. Thank You for letting us have her here with us for a time. She has left footprints on my heart."

*It was the afternoon recess when they played football with Mr. Ray most every day; an experience unriveled anywhere else in David's world!*

# Angels in Their Midst

On a dark, cold, and rainy winter's night, the police cruiser rounded the corner into the crime-infested neighborhood of the Heights. The sergeant checked the clock; it was 3:45 a.m. The cloud-covered darkness drew in the clapboard buildings closer, crowding in on the already narrow alleyways. Stormy shadows danced through the trees spawning a school of secret dangers in the sergeant's mind.

He switched on his spotlight. Then he scanned the light over scattered cars parked helter-skelter across the grassless, muddy front yards between the tightly packed, neglected ramshackle houses. His anxious eyes played tricks on him, darting nervously about through the unfamiliar neighborhood masked in darkness.

Guarded unrest in the deepest corners of his mind triggered fears that often populate the dark night, bringing the unnerving paranoia of unseen eyes peering at him through the wind-whipped shadows.

"Curse my luck for getting this call," he muttered to himself. He knew he wasn't wanted here. When people are engaged in something they are not proud of they seldom welcome witnesses. The police were the enemy in this neighborhood.

"To these people I am an intruder, the very cause of their troubled lives," he muttered to himself. "Well, I don't like it here either, in your seedy, crime infested part of town. Just my luck to suffer the deadly consequences of an unlucky witness."

Suddenly he saw movement in a beat and battered Plymouth Station Wagon. He trained the spotlight. The eyes of the assailant frozen in the light reflected back at him. The sergeant's heart quickened.

He stepped out of the cruiser, ignoring the mud as it oozed around his freshly polished shoes. Slowly and carefully, he walked the distance to the vehicle.

"Don't move," he shouted while pulling his gun. "Put your hands on the dashboard! Do it NOW!"

He walked slowly up to the vehicle. *This is just a boy*, he thought as he looked through the windshield, *but boys, too, can be dangerous in this neighborhood.*

He motioned for the boy to roll down the window. With a stern, cold stare, he questioned the boy, "What are you doing here? In the rain, in the middle of the night?"

The boy's words wrestled their way through a nervous uneasiness. "I'm waiting for my dad, sir," the boy said, "to take me to swim practice."

"Swim practice, in the middle of the night? Step out of the car," the Sergeant ordered. "Put your hands on the hood. Keep 'em visible now." He put his gun away, then pushed the boy hard against the station wagon with his left hand. He padded him down with his right.

It was then that David's father stepped through the broken screen door and out of the shadows. "Can I help you officer?" he snapped.

Startled, the sergeant turned to face him. He hadn't expected this sudden appearance and was caught off guard. "Is this your boy?" the sergeant asked in surprise. "He says you're takin' him to swimming practice?"

"That's right, sergeant," David's father snarled with a sharp edge in his voice.

Without a word the officer turned and headed back toward the police cruiser. Glancing down at his mud-caked shoes and mud-splattered pleated trousers, he muttered to no one in particular, "In the middle of a cold, rainy January night, he's goin' swimming? It's no wonder these people live in the Heights!"

✳ ✳ ✳

David was not sure his father even finished high school before joining the Marines and heading to Okinawa to fight the Japanese. But when he returned from the war in the Pacific, marred forever by the experience, he had one all-encompassing dream: to play major league baseball. It had kept him going through the life-altering experience of that whole hellacious war.

He had hoped living in this crime-infested part of town would be only temporary. Unfortunately, after ten years in the minors, having only spent time enough in "the bigs for a cup of coffee," as he put it, that chapter in his life was over. The spark of his dream had been extinguished by the realities of life and with it his passion for life seemed to vanish. He was left with no motivation, no dreams, no goals, no education, no money, seemingly few prospects, and feeling the victim of life's misfortunes.

He was now selling shoes part time, picking up occasional odd jobs, and struggling to accept his fate. Frustrated and disillusioned, he often slipped away for more than a few beers, often by himself and sometimes with his old baseball buddies to talk of the past and of the experiences of war seared into his mind forever.

✳✳✳

The anticipated glamour and celebrity David's mom, Eileen, had expected when she married a professional baseball player had long since vanished, and with its loss came the harsh realities of a difficult life, financial distress, and the contentious relationship with her husband and his unwillingness to take responsibility for his family. Eileen drove a delivery truck selling eggs in up-scale neighborhoods across town just to put food on the table, but it wasn't enough. The mortgage was always past due, creditors hounded them constantly, and she had to suffer the humiliation of the young grocery clerk telling her he could accept only cash from Eileen. Constantly disappointed by David's father, often feeling she was in this alone, she had a difficult time just feeding her children, keeping them in shoes and clothes, and showing any charity at all toward him.

Whenever or wherever the paths of David's parents happened to cross, it was WWII all over again. They fought winter, summer, spring, and fall, like cats and dogs that even a fire hose couldn't separate.

It seemed to Eileen her husband's view of the entire world was through the prism of sports, and frankly she didn't really care much at all for sports. But she didn't like the gangs in their neighborhood, either, so she grudgingly accepted the former for her son. She was well aware that David's involvement in athletics provided another justification for her husband to slip out of the house, but under cover of the white flag of a mitigated truce.

Swim meets and ballgames down at the park, all authorized by Sergeant Mom, filled David's life. But in those years following baseball, the mind of David's dad was never really in the present, he seldom spoke to David before dropping him off and disappearing for the rest of the day with unheralded but frequent stops at the bar for a beer. It was often well into the night before Eileen would see him again.

David didn't care a wit about school—"reading, writing, or arithmetic was for those who couldn't run the football or swim a lap of butterfly," he would tell his buddies. He looked on school as pure drudgery. The classroom was a purgatory to suffer through, to endure between recesses until he could get outside to play on the ball field with his buddies. Every day he stared at the clock on the schoolroom wall, counting down the minutes until that school bell rang and the prison gates of the classroom opened, letting him outside to play.

"As long as they don't hold me back a grade or stop me from playing with my buddies, I'm good," he told his best friend, Corky. Still, if not for the hour-long after-lunch recess, David and Corky would have played hooky from school most days.

It was in the fourth grade when David met Mr. Ray, his first male teacher. Mr. Ray, who in David's mind was the absolute finest teacher to ever walk planet Earth, would change David's life forever. He played softball, basketball, dodgeball, and volleyball with the boys most every at recess. But it was the long afternoon recess when they played football with Mr. Ray that kept David in school, an experience unrivaled anywhere else in his world.

Mr. Ray had an amazing arm that could cover the length of the field for those long passes, bringing David fame and glory in the end zone. He idolized Mr. Ray.

One weekend in November, David confiscated a T-shirt from each of his buddies, scrounged together what money he could, then stenciled "Ray's Guerillas" across the front of every T-shirt, with each boy's last name on the back. It was to celebrate their sandlot football team and set them apart from all the other kids on the playground as Mr. Ray's special boys. "The Crew," they called themselves.

All through the fall they played football during the afternoon recess. Then came Christmas vacation. It was pure service beyond the call of duty when Mr. Ray informed the Crew they would be playing in the first ever "Christmas Holiday Classic." Mr. Ray and a few other teachers from the Robla School District had organized a football tournament to include all five schools in a series of games during the holidays just after Christmas. It would become the most important event of the year as far as the Crew was concerned.

Looking back many years later, the grown members of the Crew realized that it wasn't quite the amazing event the boys took it to be, but to David and his buddies, it made all the difference. For the first time he wanted to please a teacher who had taken such an interest in him on the sports field, what he loved most in all of the world.

Because David for once was excited about a school event, Eileen, in an effort to be supportive, volunteered to help. Over the two weeks before Christmas she and Constance, Mr. Ray's wife, prepared drinks and refreshments and took on responsibility for anything that needed to be done outside of football. Of course they often talked and Eileen let Constance know how appreciative she was for her and her husband and how much this opportunity meant to her son.

The two mothers spent hours together each day during the weeks that followed. They grew very close to one another. From their daily conversations Constance gleaned bits of information about Eileen's circumstances. Nothing in particular really, but when put all together she surmised life was very difficult for Eileen and her family. Although Constance didn't want to meddle, she just assumed the children would be facing a bleak Christmas that year.

For her part, Eileen admired Constance and was reluctant to mention her husband's lack of steady work, their heavy debt, or any of the other problems at home. In fact, much of what little money they did earn never reached her home, and while she saw little of her meager earnings, she saw even less of her husband's time. Then one day Mr. Ray sent David home from practice with his shoes wrapped in duct tape just to keep them on. It was the proverbial last straw that broke the camel's back. Eileen went into her bedroom, closed the door behind her, leaned against it, slid down to the floor, and broke down in tears. She sat all alone on the floor crying in frustration and humiliation.

That night, when Constance called to go over the next day's schedule, Eileen told her the whole of it, including the fact they did not even have the bare necessities at home. "I'm ironing on patches over patches on David's pants. We're eating macaroni and cheese every night for dinner. And I can't even buy him new shoes for school," Eileen lamented, struggling to control her emotions. "The worst of it, my husband seems completely disengaged. Wallowing in his own struggles, he offers little help at home. I can't bear to think of our Christmas this year!"

Eileen shared that there would be nothing for Christmas, except the two dresses she had been sewing for her girls for weeks. For David, these two weeks playing football would be his only Christmas present. Her heart was full of sorrow, for there was nothing to even fill the stockings with on Christmas morning.

"I wish there was more for David. He is far too gloomy for such a young boy," Eileen shared with Constance. "He worries about the family and about our needs and neglects his own I think. I can't even buy him a pair of new shoes," she broke down crying. "I am so sorry to unburden myself on you Constance, but I have no one else to talk to. My parents have long since passed and there is no one else; please forgive me. You and your husband have been so kind to David and my family. I am so much in your debt. I can never repay you!"

Constance said little. Frankly she didn't know what to say. She thought it best to be a good listener to her new friend and so she just listened. But long after she had hung up the phone, she questioned that tactic as she rolled the conversation over and over in her mind. That night she tossed and turned as she lay in her bed unable to sleep, replaying Eileen's story again and again.

❈ ❈ ❈

Late on Christmas Eve as her children lay in their beds, Eileen sat in the front room sewing dresses for her two girls by the light of the fire to save precious electricity. She had hoped she might get a bit of satin and lace, but gingham was all she could afford. Now after midnight she was putting the final stitches onto the dresses.

Eileen's heart was so full of sorrow and concern, she felt it would surely break. Her two girls had been singing and dancing earlier in the evening as they hung their stockings on the mantle, sure that Santa would come and fill them with gifts of candy. But nine-year-old David sat alone in the corner of the cold, three-room house with a scowl on his face.

"David, look what Cathy and I made for Santa," his younger sister said, trying to cheer him up. "It's a muffin, and we're gonna leave him some milk too."

David just smiled at her, then stepped into the kitchen to confront his Mom. "Why do you encourage the girls, let them act this way, Mom?" David asked, well aware that there was nothing for Christmas and Santa was but a hoax. "It just builds up their hopes. Then when no Santa comes, they are gonna be twice as disappointed."

David had become very cynical; his childhood fantasies and hope for the future had been pushed out of his mind. How it broke Eileen's heart!

"David, please let them at least have their moment," she kindly responded. "What can it hurt to allow them an evening of hope, anticipation, and enjoyment? The winter has just started and soon enough it will be cold and harsh for them. Let it go, David."

David just turned away. Times were hard for his mom, and David knew it. Being the oldest he felt a kind of responsibility for protecting his sister and orphaned cousin. *And sometimes*, he thought as he looked back into the kitchen at her working there, *Mom too. She looks so worried.*

Eileen had helped her two girls hang their darned and mended stockings, but she could not persuade David to participate. All David would say in response to her encouragement was, "Mom, please don't do this; don't ask me to pretend. I'm sorry, I just can't!"

After the stockings had been hung, Eileen read the Christmas story "'Twas the Night before Christmas," then sent the children to bed.

"Aw, do we have to, Mom?" her youngest pleaded. "Can't we just stay awake for Santa? I so want to see what he brings us!"

But, of course, Eileen would have none of it and hustled them all off to bed. The girls snuggled deep into the covers of their shared bed as Eileen tucked them in. They were smiling and still so excited. Eileen leaned down and kissed them both good night, quickly wiping away a tear as she did. Then she turned to David, who lay quietly on his side facing the wall. She kissed him on his cheek. "Good night, David. I love you!"

He said nothing in response.

❋ ❋ ❋

Eileen sat in front of a dying fire sewing the two dresses for her girls, her eyes straining in the dim light of the fire. She put her needle aside for a moment. Stretching out her arms and arching her back after hours of painstaking work, she leaned back against the chair. Everyone was in

bed now; she was all alone with her thoughts. Tears began again, trick-
ling down her cheeks as the melancholy set in. "This will be a Christmas
to remember, all right," she said to herself, "and I am not looking forward to remembering it."

Eileen finished her last stitch on the dresses, then looked up at the
clock. It was well after one in the morning. The fire was almost out and it
was getting cold in the house. She looked at the little mended stockings
still hanging empty, wondering what she might put in them. Eileen felt
desolate in her heart.

She stood, began collecting her things, and prepared to hang the two
dresses, when she heard something out in the front yard. Eileen looked
through the window. Outside the wind was blowing hard and cold, but
she could see someone on her front porch.

Uneasily, she turned on the porch light and opened the front door,
catching the intruders off guard. And there stood Constance in the
light, with her husband and two children behind her all with a surprised look on their faces. They had been caught red handed, cold and
shivering. Eileen just stood there looking at them, without a word, not
yet registering what was happening. Then she saw the packages in their
arms and tears came to her eyes. Her friends had come on Christmas
morning to change the lives of her family.

Constance reached out for her and took Eileen in her arms. "Merry
Christmas," she said.

"Oh, Constance, you have already done so much for us. How can I
ever thank you and your family?" Eileen tearfully said.

"You already have, Eileen," she said. "You already have!"

Finally coming to her senses, "I'm so sorry. It's cold out here. Please
come into the house." Smiling and wiping away a tear of her own,
Constance introduced Eileen to her two little girls. "These are my daughters, Elsa and Jenny."

"Hello!" the cute little girls both responded at the same time.

"And a hello to you," Eileen answered back. "You look so pretty in
your Christmas dresses."

Each picked up their packages ready to bring them inside. Eileen
swung open the door and steppe aside so they might enter.

When Constance and her family entered the home, it was then the
presents of Christmas became the miracle of Christmas. Each looked

around and saw how bare and stark it was and knew why they had come. Constance, with a tear in her eye knew why she had felt so urgently inspired to forego their own Christmas and share their blessings with this family.

Each child had picked their favorite present to donate, a gift they treasured and would rather keep for themselves, with Mom and Dad throwing in a little extra to make it a real Christmas for Eileen's family. It had been their intention to leave them all at the front door anonymously, but when caught in the act, of course the plan had changed.

The girls looked tenderly at a favorite doll and a magnificent play-house with all its many parts. Then each placed their beautiful doll, playhouse, and packages on the bare floor, in the near empty front room of the cold, shadowy, and uninviting single room that lodged their living, kitchen, and everything else room. Only the two bedrooms were upstairs.

Eileen switched on the light, revealing clean but well-worn walls, floors, and sparse furnishings. She insisted they all stand by the stove while she warmed up a little hot chocolate, and they warmed their hands over the extra flame. Eileen, still wiping tears from her eyes began to laugh at the absurdity of the scene, all standing around a single flame to get warm. They all joined in with her laughter, as the spirit of Christmas warmed their hearts.

It was nearly three in the morning when the Ray family left. Eileen hurried around filling stockings, placing gifts at their most strategic angles, then lighting another fire in the hearth. There was a Christmas ham and all the fixings for a fine Christmas dinner.

As she opened the cardboard-wrapped packages to discover the contents in each, she felt giddy as a schoolgirl. Then she found a note left in one: "Thank you for the best Christmas we have ever had. We hope you and your family have a very Merry Christmas!"

※ ※ ※

The family awakened to the Christmas miracle just before sunrise, about the time Eileen finished her work and should have been ready for bed. But the excitement of the morning and the exhilaration of their good fortune so filled her heart that there was no way she could sleep. There was a fire in the hearth. Bacon was sizzling on the stove. Hot muffins were ready to come out of the oven. The jams, precious honey, jellies, and fruit, fruit everywhere! There was the spirit of Christmas filling every corner of their little home.

Her husband was the first to come down. Eileen couldn't help herself and gave him a big welcoming hug. "What's that for, Eileen?" he asked, not yet seeing the miracle that had taken hold of their Christmas morning.

"Oh, just because I remembered how much I love you," she responded. "You know I have always loved you?"

He looked at her cautiously, waiting for the other shoe to drop, then turned, looking around the little downstairs room, the presents, the full stockings, the Christmas ham. He was speechless as he turned back toward Eileen, "What happened here?" he asked, disbelieving his own eyes.

With a wink and a smile, "Christmas!" was her only response.

And he hugged her back. "I'm so sorry, Eileen. Things are gonna change around here. I promise." Then he kissed her to seal the promise.

The girls came down the stairs, rubbing the sleep from their eyes, until they saw their stockings hanging from the mantle, so full with candy and treats it looked as if they might fall to the floor at any moment. Hanging next to their stockings were their two dresses, which each grabbed and with bright, wide eyes and infectious smiles that made Eileen tear up once again, only this time with joy in her heart. They each held up their new dresses tight to their shoulders, then spun around the room singing and dancing in delight.

With the warmth of the fire in the hearth and the smell the bacon, eggs, muffins, and sweet jams wafting through the air, the two girls squealed with pleasure. "Look at all of Santa's presents. Do you see them, Mom? Do you see them?"

Finally, the last to wake, David slowly came down the stairs, head hung down, a frown scrunching up his boyish face. "What's all the racket?" he grumbled in his best "bah, humbug" Scrooge voice. "You woke me up."

It wasn't until the very last step on the stairs, when the greatest miracle of all happened. He looked up, rubbed his lying eyes in disbelief as he looked at the location where Mom had hung his stocking. He didn't hear his sisters scream at him in delight. He didn't see the tears running down Eileen's cheeks as she looked on at him, nor see his father's smile of proud recognition.

The cold light of daybreak streamed silently through the window, settling softly on the most beautiful sight David had ever seen in his long nine years of life. It just hung there next to his crammed and bulging Christmas stocking there in vibrant blue, with silver stitching, trimmed in gold. He recognized it the moment he saw it, for he had admired it on many an occasion, hanging up behind glass in Mr. Ray's office. David would recognize that gold number-12 college football jersey anywhere. It was Mr. Ray's, the most beautiful thing in all the world.

"What is this, Mom?" David asked, stunned, still not believing his own eyes, the emotion clearly evident in the halting catch of his voice.

"It's Christmas, David," she said with tears steaming down her cheeks. "It is a Merry Christmas for our family!"

That morning a childhood had been brought back to life, a young boy with all the hopes and dreams for the future and a renewed belief in the miracle of Christmas. All the lives in a family had been changed for the better by simple gifts from angels in their midst.

※ ※ ※

The miracle of hope offered on that Christmas holiday marked a turning point in the life of this little family. David's father found permanent work, put the past behind him, and was good to his word to Eileen. With the household financial obligations and family responsibilities becoming a shared commitment, tension and tempers eased.

And David? Well, David would be forever grateful. He could not disappoint Mr. Ray on the sports field and after that Christmas, he couldn't bear to disappoint him in the classroom either. The change in attitude transformed his very outlook on life and of course, his future.

Most of David's buddies from the Heights were to be in and out of juvenile hall during the years that followed. Some eventually ended up in prison. Most of the girls had babies before they finished high school. But it was Mr. Ray and his family who let David see that maybe, just maybe, he could get more out of life if he put as much effort into his schooling as he did onto the sports field.

It was a difficult transformation for David, but Mr. Ray let him know he could and should do as Henry Ford suggested, "Whether you think you can, or you think you can't—you're right."[1]

David owed Mr. Ray a debt of gratitude he could never repay for the gift he and his family had been given. That year of David's life with Mr. Ray was never forgotten. But gratitude never spoken is like a gift wrapped, but never delivered.[2] Many years later, while visiting Sacramento with his wife and young children of his own, on yet another Christmas holiday, David tracked down Mr. Ray who had become the Robla School District's Superintendent of Schools, changing boys lives for forty years in the same under-privileged minority neighborhood. He still recalled those days of Ray's Guerillas and the gift of that special Christmas.

Said the author Harriet Beecher Stowe, "The bitterest tears shed over graves are for the words left unsaid and deeds left undone."[3] Thank you—it is such a simple phrase, but with profound meaning to the receiver. I was honored to offer Mr. Ray a sincere "Thank you, for the gift your family, truly angels in our midst, gave my family on that long-ago Christmas!"

*It was spring cleaning like no other: a dozen work parties, five supersized dumpsters, and hundreds of hours donated. Jenny's home and her world began to spring to life.*

# Serve One Another

ain first raised the question, Am I my brother's keeper? Are we responsible to look after the wellbeing of our neighbors as we go about our daily lives? The Lord's answer is the same today as it was then, a resounding "Yes, we are." Unfortunately, much of the world follows the admonition of Cain and says, "No, we are not."

Who is our brother? Who is our neighbor? We are surrounded by those in need of our attention, our encouragement, our support, our comfort, and our kindness. Our Savior entrusted us to become His hands here upon the earth, charged with the mandate to serve and lift His children where we can. He is counting on each of us. We may lament, "I can barely make it through each day, doing all that I need to do. How can I provide service to others? What can I possibly do? How can I justify pulling myself away from my own family with so little time available to touch even one life?"

I would like to share with you a story of one of our neighbors here in our little corner of the world, one life touched by a caring friend, a family, a congregation.

Jenny had not set foot out in public during the bright light of day in more than a quarter century. She had long since slipped from productive member of society to casual observer, then drifted to the sidelines of life, withdrawn from friends, from visitors, and finally from any kind of productive life altogether. There had been concern from her church where she had attended many years before, from the community where she lived, and from family who lived thousands of miles away. But most of those who had reached out to her had been pushed away and long since given up. The barriers were too high.

With no phone, no TV, no family to care for or support her, she had closed her door on the world and slipped into a hermit's life. Now even her two cats had long since passed away.

Except for an infrequent predawn trip to the grocery store and an occasional church visitor who was never allowed to enter her home, she had no human contact. For decades, Jenny had succumbed to a life as a voluntary prisoner alone in her own home, with infrequent books and the quiet musings of her own mind to keep her company as she sank deeper into depression. She lost all interest in her appearance and hygiene, and she lived amongst the filth of her own making—a hoarder, a recluse, a lost soul.

To say she was lonely didn't do her condition justice, really. She had given up on life and although still relatively young, she was slipping away. What did it matter to the world if she quietly slipped from this life and on to the next?

Well it mattered to Brent, a caring friend from her congregation. He understood Christ's calling for him and all of us, to care for our neighbor. As he put it, "Charity is not a passive acceptance or tolerance of people. It is truly feeling the love of God and doing our best to translate it into love for one another," he said, in an effort to solicit help from the rest of his congregation. "It is a sincere concern for our neighbor that draws them toward the blessings of the gospel of Christ, more than anything else we do."

The Apostle Paul knew this love, and he saw people that way. It was a part of who he was. When he went forth, thousands were drawn to his compassionate caring and to the gospel of Jesus Christ.

It had been far too long since Jenny had felt the love of Christ and that of her church family, so Brent committed himself and encouraged John, a gruff but valiant and compassionate friend from the congregation, to join him. Brent and John set a single goal to be accomplished with Jenny: "Break down the barriers Jenny has so long labored to build and allow us to help her return to the loving kindness and comforting arms of her Savior and caring church family."

Step by step, through months of patient caring and longsuffering kindness, those barriers were eroded. Then one day, the long-standing question was posed yet again, "Jenny, will you let us help you?"

In a moment of surrender, she let her guard down. Her eyes moistened in pain. Then with tears streaming down her face, the words struggled through her shyness, "Could you please?"

The Apostle Paul admonished, "By love serve one another."[1] The Savior's entire ministry exemplified love of neighbor. The blind man He healed, the daughter of Jarus He raised, lepers He cleansed, and the woman at the well He taught—all were neighbors of Jesus. They may not have been of His faith, but He reached out to all in need nonetheless. He, the perfect man, stood before sinners and extended a hand. And so the caravan of His kindness went on to His neighbors. It serves as an example to us all, as it did to these two wonderful kind men and their families, and to the congregation who stepped up to love and care for Jenny in her time of need.

No one had entered Jenny's home in more than fifteen years when John and Brent crossed that threshold into a world of human tragedy. The scene before them was horrific. The smell even more so. It was an indescribable assault on the senses. There had been no power, nor running water in a dozen years. No trash had been collected in even longer.

Trash was piled outside and flowed into the halls of her home that led to now inaccessible and useless rooms. Diffused light peppered the spider-web-covered walls through holes in a roof that had not served its purpose for more than a decade.

How had a member of the community, of the congregation, inactive or not, been allowed to sink so low? All of God's children have the gift of agency, but how often do we live side by side, but never communicate heart to heart with those who quietly cry out for our help? It was hard to imagine Jenny living just down the road from the church under such horrific conditions.

John, Brent, their families, and many others in the congregation were about to change Jenny's life and in the process enrich their own lives. As Christ taught, "For whosoever shall save his life shall lose it: but whosoever shall lose his life for my sake and the gospel's, the same shall save it."[2] Is not the Savior telling us that those who live only for themselves eventually shrivel up and lose the fullness of life, while those who lose themselves in the service of others grow and flourish? Those who serve Christ relish the abundance of life's blessings offered during their time on earth and in effect save their own lives.

\* \* \*

Though their goal was to clean and weatherproof Jenny's home before the worst of the winter was upon them, Jenny was not sure she was prepared for the painful changes in her life. She told herself she was ready for the help, but to have people in her life again was very distressing, unnerving, and upsetting. She was frightened and afraid to let down her guard, to be a cooperative participant in change.

It was gradual at first. Little by little, Jenny relinquished access to her home to these good men and their families. She allowed them to begin the process of clearing away the cobwebs and debris from both her home and her mind. She allowed them to help her. Slowly and steadily, one step at a time, they began to turn Jenny's house back into a home again and bring her back into the kind and caring fold of Christ.

Eleven-year-old Emma, who lived with her family just around the corner, watched Jenny from the sidelines on that first day of work. She felt compassion for the anxious and agitated Jenny sitting at the backyard garden table alone, wringing her hands. The next day, Emma brought her new puppy, Abby, who took to Jenny immediately. Instinctively, Abby gravitated toward the frightened, nervous, uneasy Jenny as she struggled to allow strangers into her house to move and throw away her things.

Abby was sensitive and kind, and she brought an involuntary smile to Jenny's face, calming and comforting her nerves and allowing her to relax as the work progressed on her house. Emma and Abby came over and kept Jenny company each day during the reconstruction of her home and her life.

A smile would come to Jenny's face as soon as the two of them walked through the gate each afternoon. It was not long before Jenny and Abby became best of friends, and Jenny was asking Emma if it might be all right for Abby to stay the night. Each day the bond between Abby and Jenny grew stronger, until Jenny had Abby for sleepovers most every night.

At first it was only Abby that could bring a smile to Jenny's face, but in time she grew attached to Emma as well. Day after day during the weeks separating Thanksgiving and Christmas, Emma walked down to Jenny's after school, and soon on weekends too, and then over the holidays to work on their family project. Often Emma worked not just with her own family, but others from the congregation as well. During that time Jenny became as close to Emma as she had to anyone in decades. They talked about anything and everything, and each day the bond between Jenny, Abby, and Emma grew stronger.

Gradually, Jenny opened up to others as well and became more comfortable with many of the families in the congregation that came to work on her home. She began to express her appreciation, her thankfulness, her gratitude for all they were doing for her. And on Sundays when no one came to work, she missed their company.

It was a spring-cleaning like no other. More than a dozen work parties, five supersized dumpsters, and hundreds of hours donated by these two men, their families, other members of the congregation, and many grateful neighbors transformed a house and brought a woman back from the outer edge of society. Jenny's home and her world began to spring to life. There was a new roof, a refurbished kitchen, a bathroom with running water, and a bedroom with a real bed. There were volunteers from every quarter. As Emma's mom said, "The service we have rendered as a family has brought us closer together and helped my children appreciate all that the Lord has given us."

The work was finished just before Christmas, and one by one, all the families who had worked on Jenny's home offered their final Christmas greetings and a wish for the very best to Jenny. Each better understood the blessings of service to one another, the value of the loving touch of a grateful hand, and the beauty of a communal family living the gospel of Christ. There were tears shed by many over those last couple of days of work. Jenny would miss many of them.

❄ ❄ ❄

When all was said and done, Emma's family stopped by on Saturday afternoon, the day before Christmas to offer Christmas hugs and greetings to Jenny. Since they lived just around the block, each promised to stop by from time to time. Jenny had tears in her eyes as she hugged each member of the family.

Then to everyone's surprise Emma handed Abby's leash to Jenny. "I want you to have her, Jenny" Emma said. "More importantly, Abby wants you to have her as well. She loves you more than anyone else in this world and you deserve each other. I saw it from the very beginning."

With tears in her eyes, all Jenny could muster was a sweet smile and said, "Thank you, Emma!"

"Of course you couldn't be happy without her, Jenny, when she needs you so." Emma smiled back. "If it's okay I'll stop by to see her, and you and I can talk about things!" There were no more words from Jenny, only tears of tenderness, compassion, and joy streaming down her face.

✳ ✳ ✳

Life is a long road, but after more than a quarter century, Jenny stepped back into church on a Christmas Sunday, once again feeling the warmth and affection of the human touch, the spontaneous smile that comes from the laughter of little children and the love of her neighbors in their patient practice of the gospel of Christ. And of course the companionship and love for her Abby and a never-ending gratitude and admiration for a young girl's compassionate gift.

The challenges for Jenny in her new life had just begun, but at least she was on the path with her Savior there to hold her hand.

In the words of Christ in the twenty-fifth chapter of Matthew: "Come, ye blessed of my Father, inherit the kingdom prepared for you from the foundation of the world: For I was an hungred, and ye gave me meat: I was thirsty, and ye gave me drink: I was a stranger, and ye took me in: Naked, and ye clothed me: I was sick, and ye visited me: I was in prison, and ye came unto me."[3]

"Then shall the righteous answer him, saying, Lord, when saw we thee and hungered, and fed thee? Or thirsty, and gave thee drink? When saw we thee a stranger, and took thee in? Or naked, and clothed thee? Or saw we thee sick, or in prison, and came unto thee?"[4] And Christ answered and said to them "Verily I say unto you, Inasmuch as ye have done it unto one of the least of these my brethren, ye have done it unto me."[5]

*The busy, impatient innkeeper was short and curt in his response as he abruptly turned Joseph and Mary away. "There is no room for you here in my inn."*

# The Spirit of Christmas

*T*here is an old story often told during the Christmas season about an innkeeper in Bethlehem at the time of Christ's birth. Because of the census that was being taken under the order of Roman Emperor, Cesar Augustus, the roads were crowded with people traveling to the cities of their birth. All the inns in the City of David, Bethlehem, were full to overflowing. In particular, this old innkeeper was kept busy running here and there, attending to the needs of his little family business. Like many of us in our busy lives, there was not time to do all the things that were demanded of him. He grew anxious and frustrated. And still more travelers came, looking for accommodations that night.

A young couple came to the door of his inn from far away in Galilee on that long ago. "There were two who came to the inn—a husband and a wife—whom the innkeeper would not have turned away for all the gold and silver in the world, had he known who they were."[1]

Mary, already suffering the early pains of labor, waited outside in the evening cold as Joseph told the innkeeper, "My wife is carrying a child, and she can travel no further." The busy, impatient innkeeper was short and curt in his response as he abruptly turned them away. "There is no room for you here in the inn."

As Matthew tells us, the only lodging this desperate, anxious couple could find was in a manger. A crude cave cut into the hillside where the animals were kept.

And so it was that while they were there among the animals, Mary delivered a beautiful baby boy, her firstborn son, the Son of Man. She "wrapped him in swaddling clothes, and laid him in a manger; because there was no room for them in the inn,"[2] Luke declares. With heavenly hosts singing, "Glory to God in the highest, and on earth peace, good will toward men,"[3] the shepherds came with tidings of great joy to see the babe, and to bear Him gifts and then praised God for all the things they had seen and heard.

The innkeeper had missed the greatest opportunity in generations of life on earth. "Long years afterward, it would not do any good for him to repeat over and over again the words, 'If only I had known who they were, I would have made room for them.'"[4]

What wouldn't he give to recant that irreversible decree that lead Mary to lay the Christ child in the rude manger, because there was no room in his inn? No room? No room for the Son of Man?

Today we have beautiful homes with rooms for dining, rooms for sleeping, rooms for study, rooms for play, but for many there is no room for Christ in our home or in our lives.

Recall with me Jesus's own words, "Foxes have holes, and birds of the air have nests; but the Son of man hath not where to lay his head."[5] There is so much competition for our attention in our lives that sometimes we forget to make room for Christ, to find room for Him in our home.

"Born in a stable, cradled in a manger, He came forth from heaven to live on earth as mortal man and to establish the kingdom of God. During His earthly ministry, He taught men the higher law. His glorious gospel reshaped the thinking of the world. He blessed the sick. He caused the lame to walk, the blind to see, the deaf to hear. He even raised the dead to life."[6] He provided the light, the life, the way, a power stronger than weapons, a wealth more lasting than the coins of Caesar. His gospel reshaped the thinking of the entire world.

What was the reaction to His message of mercy, His words of wisdom, His lessons of life? There were a precious few, who in His own time appreciated Him for who He was. They bathed His feet. They learned His words. They followed His example.

But most did not appreciate Him for the gifts of the spirit He offered. Aldous Huxley wrote, "Most human beings have an almost infinite capacity to take their blessings for granted."[7] Human nature was no different in Jesus's time.

Some treated Him as an enemy, a traitor, less than human. He was mocked in what some called a trial. Angry shouts of "Crucify Him! Crucify Him!" heightened the tension of the night. And when the cock crowed, His prophecy was sealed on Peter's head.

Peter who would be the cornerstone of Christ's church, the rock, wept in anguish and disillusioned despair, staggering alone into the dawn, as his Christ commenced the long climb up Calvary's hill.

Jesus was nailed to a cross amid humiliating cries of "If he be the King of Israel, let him now come down from the cross, and we will believe him. . . . He saved others; himself he cannot save."[8]

The Son of Man, the Christ, our Savior withstood all, that He might meet His commitment to His Father in Heaven. He suffered, bled, and was crucified to atone for the sins of all mankind—for you and for me.

Without a hint of guile or retribution His final words on this earth: "Father, forgive them; for they know not what they do."[9]

"Into thy hands I commend my spirit."[10]

The Son of Man passed from this life as light around the world went out. He was lowered from the cross. His disfigured, lifeless body left naked on the ground in blaspheme.

With unimaginable anguish His mother, John the Beloved, and loved ones gathered Him up, wrapped his body, then placed Him in a sepulcher offered-up by a converted soul, a member of the very Sanhedrin court who condemned to death their Yeshua.

Christ's disciples were left confused, bewildered, and scared as they stumbled through the long tempestuous night. Most must have wandered the city alone with Christ's lingering admonition still ringing in their ears, "Fear thou not, for I am with thee; be not dismayed; for I am thy God; I will strengthen thee; yea, I will help thee; yea, I will uphold thee with the right hand of my righteousness."[11] How could it be? How could He have left me here alone? What did He mean?

Thunder and darkness covered the whole earth. It trembled and shook in pain. Finally the angry clouds spilled a cleansing rain to wipe away that terrible night.

※ ※ ※

Very early on a crisp, quiet, beautiful Sunday morning, a heartbroken Mary came to the sepulchre to find His body gone. The world would never be the same—for Jesus Christ had broken the bonds of death. "He had risen." "Weeping may endure for a night, but joy cometh in the morning."[12]

Now for the first time, the eyes of His disciples could see, their ears could hear, and their hearts could feel and understand the full mission of their Savior—the greatest miracle of all time, giving each of us the opportunity to be resurrected with Him in the beautiful springtime of our lives.

Down through the generations of time, the message of Jesus has been the same. "To Peter by the shores of Galilee, He said, 'Follow me.' To Philip of old came the call, 'Follow me.' And to you and me, if we but listen, will come that same beckoning invitation, 'Follow me.'"[13] If we follow in His footsteps, if we but emulate His example, we will have opportunities to bless the lives of others. Jesus invites all of us to give of ourselves "with a perfect heart and with a willing mind."[14] Our opportunities are limitless. There are hearts to be gladdened. There are gifts to be given. There are deeds to be done.

✳ ✳ ✳

Some years ago, I visited my father in a hospice home during his final days of life. Most were in this home for only a short few days before they passed beyond the veil. One early Sunday morning, while dad was sleeping, I met an old woman who had defied the odds. "More than three weeks have passed since I was left alone to die," she told me. But as she explained, lifting the curtain to peer out the window, she had no intention of passing on until her boy came to visit. She seemed to have worn out that curtain in the hope that he would come. "I think my boy will come see me today," she told me listlessly. I wondered if he would.

Who is it that awaits your visit? To whom should you be serving this Christmas? Remember what Ralph Waldo Emerson said, "Rings and jewels are not gifts but apologies for gifts; the only true gift in life is a gift of oneself."[15] "To catch the real meaning of the Spirit of Christmas, we need only drop the last syllable, and it becomes the Spirit of Christ."[16] The spirit of Christ is never found in the excess of things. It is less obvious upon arrival and more lasting in impact. It brings to our hearts impressionable warmth that has little to do with worldly goods but a whole lot to do with families, with love, with patience, with compassion, and with caring.

Let us always remember, "he who gives money gives much, he who gives time gives more, but he who gives of himself gives all."[17] If we but let it be so, the Spirit of Christ "[will illuminate] the picture window of the soul, and we [will] look out upon the world's busy life and become more interested in people than things."[18] So be kind to all you meet. For each of us carries a burden that others cannot see.

There is still time this Christmas season to extend a helping hand, a loving heart, a willing spirit. Follow the example of our Savior. Don't forfeit your opportunity, as did the innkeeper so many years ago. Don't let the passage of time leave a hole of regret in your heart that cannot be filled. Make room for Him, and make room for those in need within your heart. For with good tidings and great joy, unto us this day, a Savior was born. Show your gratitude for His gift to each of us, the greatest gift of all time, the gift of eternal life.

*With single-minded purpose, David reached deep for every bit of strength he could dredge from muscles trained over thousands of long grueling hours in the early-morning quiet, while the rest of the world still nestled snug in their beds.*

# The Biggest, Baddest
# Mad Dog in Town

*D*avid stood atop the starting block in the final moments of his preparation; eyes focused intently on fourteen-year-old teammate Jimmy Mick closing the gap on the leaders in the breaststroke leg of the 200m medley relay. Over the past year this relay team had become a force to be reckoned with, winning virtually every race entered in swim meets all over California. But that had been with Chuck Coleman swimming the butterfly leg on the relay.

Unfortunately, Chuck had turned fifteen just as David was turning thirteen, just ten days before Christmas. In the world of Age Group Swimming, Chuck was out, and David was in. With his thirteenth birthday, David had entered a brave new world where boys sprouted up like weeds with croaking voices and developing muscles—muscles you could actually see.

Just before the start of this Junior Olympic, 13–14 age group, medley relay final, their leadoff backstroker who himself was about to turn fifteen delivered a real clear message to David. With an Iron Clamp on the back of his neck and a knuckle sandwich to his forehead, came the warning, "You may think you were some kind of child phenom, but you're with the big boys now. If you mess this up, I wouldn't wanna be in your shoes . . . not with the 'Mad Dog' around." If David hadn't been under enough pressure already, that one sided interview had done it.

BBMD: the "Biggest, Baddest Mad Dog" in town, alias John Fausnaut, almost a foot taller than David and some seventy pounds of solid muscle heavier. With his scraggily goatee, a reputation of being meaner than a junk yard dog and a cold hard stare that could stop a beating heart, he looked more like old King Kong to David than the freestyle anchor on their medley relay team. There are some guys you just don't want to mess with—especially in this 1960s gangland neighborhood where the sheer brutality of enforcing Charles Darwin's "survival of the fittest" message gave that doctrine a whole new meaning. David wasn't about to do anything to bring the wrath of the "Mad Dog" down on himself, if he could help it.

He knew he was the intruder. He knew he was the weak link on their relay. It would take the swim of his life just to give the amazing John Fausnaut an opportunity to chase down the rest of the field with his blazing fast freestyle on the anchor leg of this relay. Fausnaut had already broken his own national records in the 50- and 100-meter freestyle while on his way to setting four new Junior Olympic Records earlier in this Christmas week Junior Olympic competition. It had been a sight to behold, where the power of brute lightning met the most perfect stroke ever swam by man.

Their 200m Medley Relay Team had qualified third for the final with some of the best teams in the country, filling out the rest of the competition. Santa Clara qualified first. Mark Spitz would be swimming their butterfly leg. In just four years, Spitz would set the world record in the butterfly, and then go on to win seven gold medals in the 1972 Munich Olympic Games—an Olympic gold medal count that would remain unbroken for thirty-six years until Michael Phelps entered onto the scene in 2008.

The LA Aquatic Club had qualified second in the final, and the great Harry Diaz, who had set an eleven- and twelve-year-old national record in the individual medley the year before would be swimming their butterfly leg.

David knew he just had to keep it close. He just had to, no matter what it took to do it. And now at this critical moment, he was deep in concentration preparing for the most perfect start humanly possible with his toes leaving the block just as Jimmy Mick touched the wall.

Locked and loaded with his hands pushed forward on the starting block, he made the long calculated swing into action, launching his outstretched body over Jimmy just as he touched the wall in a virtual tie with Santa Clara on the left and the LA Aquatic Club on the right.

When it's time to perform at your best, the time for preparation is over. Adrenaline coursed through David's veins, and into his very soul.

With single-minded purpose, he reached deep for every bit of strength his heart and soul could dredge from muscles trained over thousands of long grueling hours in the early morning quiet while the rest of the world still nestled snug in their beds.

Resolute in his determination to push his body beyond the limits of his own mind, David matched Diaz stroke for stroke as they went down the length of the pool. But there was really little either could do to stop Spitz from pulling well ahead. David touched the wall with nothing left in the tank, but he knew he had done his very best to keep it close setting John Fausnaut, their Achilles, off on his record breaking freestyle anchor leg. Fausnaut did what old King Kong always does. He blew away the field with terrifying power and blistering speed in a lightning fast split to bring home the gold medal.

Shocked and elated, the thrill of victory surged through the depths of his soul as the realization sank in. *We have just broken the Junior Olympic and National Age Group records. I now and will forever be a part of the record books, a member of a national record holding team—every athlete's dream.* It would never happen again in his fifteen-year swimming career with over forty thousand grueling miles of training.

As David settled into a sense of euphoria at their victory, he imagined himself on the awards podium receiving the gold medal and plaques for both the J.O. and National Records. But from the far end of the 50-meter pool, he watched as his coach approached in long, determined strides. There was an unwavering sense of purpose in his step; crimson anger spreading across his face. He was heading in David's direction. *Clearly, Coach isn't on his way to congratulate me for a job well done*, he thought. His blazing eyes and clenched jaw told a different story.

In an instant David knew his offense and the consequences for it. He was about to be charged with an indefensible act of sabotage and suffer the brutal retribution for this most unpardonable sin in the swimming world.

So desperately had he wanted to hold up his responsibility on this relay team for these older boys, he had left the starting block too early. He had jumped, snatching failure out of the jaws of victory.

Coach loomed over him. "How could you do this?" he snarled. "Do you know what you've done to your teammates? This is their final competition together."

Stunned, dazed, and still smarting from the rebuke, heartache, regret, and the "if only's" began seeping into the pit of David's stomach. He made the long walk to the locker room in front of a few hundred moms, dads, and spectators in the stands. Trying his best to maintain control of his emotions as the announcer broadcast his indiscretion over the loud speakers, he couldn't avoid hearing the chorus of "Ah, how could he do that? What was that idiot thinking?" "He just cost his teammates the gold medal and National and J.O. records? Does he realize what he's done?"

There was no safe space for David to retire to. No counselors protecting his fragile thirteen-year-old self-esteem or calming voice to tell him it would be all right. There would be no redo. No next time. No tomorrow is another day. There would be nowhere to hide his shame. It was clear that the gods of the swimming world would exact the ultimate price for this abominable act of treachery. If he was lucky, the best he could hope for was shunning from all who mattered.

David headed straight from the pool area, through the locker room, and into the seclusion of his hotel room. There he would remain sequestered for the rest of the weekend. Quarantined from the world. Holed up stuffing himself with Little Joe's cheese and pepperoni pizza and washing down his sorrows with gallons of Yogi's Cherry Slurpees. There was no consoling him. He knew his short thirteen-year-old life was over—no question about it. BBMD would see to that.

"Luckily you won't have to see John and the rest of the boys over Christmas," his dad told him. "It will give them a little time to put the loss behind them."

"I will never have to see him ever again if I have anything to do with it," he told his dad. "I'm never going back to practice again."

Unfortunately, Dad insisted that come the Monday morning after Christmas, David would have to show up at the YMCA for practice and face his fears. David tried to explain, "It would be like flaunting a red flag in front of a raging bull, an invitation for almost certain death." But like most adults, Dad just didn't get it.

"This will be the worst Christmas of my life," David told his father, "knowing that just two days after Christmas, I will be squashed like a bug."

David could think of nothing but seeing the Mad Dog after Christmas. It made for a very poor Christmas spirit. Even the presents he had looked forward to the whole year didn't seem to bring a smile. He dreaded the coming confrontation and could think of nothing else. It completely messed up his Christmas.

Monday morning arrived a lot quicker than David had hoped. But luckily, at 4:20 a.m. in the morning it was still dark, so he hid in the shadows until enough time had passed that all had gone into the pool area. Then he slipped into the locker room and sat quietly by himself, staring at the lockers.

"I just can't do it," he told himself. "I don't have the courage to face them."

Then the reverberating click of the metal door leading from the pool area and into the locker room. The echo of footsteps on the tile floor coming in David's direction.

He felt a presence. A dark shadow enveloped him as he sat on the bench hunched over, staring at the floor.

He knew it was BBMD and was equally certain of the further humiliation that was coming his way. An anxious silence filled the air, but nothing came. *He is gonna drag out the slow torture before he brutalizes me,* David thought.

Depressed, dejected, he felt a suffocating panic seize his heart. He was sure it would pound right through his chest.

The agonizing silence seemed to last a lifetime. He sat paralyzed. Anxious imagination, left unchecked ran amuck.

*Now what?* he asked in his heart. Did he really wanted to know?

The suspense was unbearable. Could it really be worse than the excruciating humiliation of waiting in anticipation?

*Yeah, it could!* he thought

Feeling entirely and utterly alone, David pleaded, "Say something. Anything! Whatever it's gonna be, please, just get it over with."

※ ※ ※

Even when we put forth our best effort we often struggle, sometimes stumble, and sometimes fail. Sometimes things turn out so very disappointingly or just downright awful—spinning out of control with seemingly no light at the end of the tunnel. But as Shakespeare put it, "Our fears do make us traitors."[1] You cannot allow your fears to rule over you;

they are traitors. Often you lose the good you might have won because you are too afraid to make the attempt.

We must learn to deal with and control our fears. If you want to be successful at anything in life, you must be willing to struggle, overcome fear of failure, and the inevitable consequences that may come with it. We cannot succumb to fear, for there is only one way to achieve success: take the leap, and pray to God you can fly.

There will always be those who find reasons why success is just not possible, nor worth the risk or the struggle. But then there is more to life than watching other people live it, just because we can't see clearly through the fog of our fears. The simple fact is, what we often call "Lucky breaks in life" look a whole lot like hard work and a willingness to risk failure.

Of course, there are no guarantees in life. "If you want a guarantee," as Clint Eastwood put it, "buy a toaster."[1] Life is relentless. It's out of fear of failure and avoidance of struggle that so many are attracted to the sweetness of illusion rather than face the harshness of reality. Harry Emerson wrote, "One of the widest gaps in human experience is the gap between what we say we want to be and our willingness to discipline ourselves to get there."[2]

To quote President Teddy Roosevelt:

> It is not the critic who counts, not the man who points out how the strong man stumbled, or where the doer of deeds could have done better. The credit belongs to the man who is actually in the arena; whose face is marred by the dust and sweat and blood; who strives valiantly; who errs and comes short again and again, because there is no effort without error or shortcoming; who knows the great enthusiasms, the great devotions and spends himself in a worthy cause; who at the best, knows in the end the triumph of high achievement, and who, at worst, if he fails, at least fails while daring greatly; so that his place shall never be with those cold and timid souls who know neither victory or defeat.[3]

When we discipline ourselves to face life's challenges head on, resolute, with the requisite struggle to become proficient and have the fortitude to overcome the inevitable obstacles in our path, we build the character that makes the heart, mind, and soul grow stronger.

Sometimes we fail, but this too teaches us to face our fears and the consequences of our choices—it's called character building. The struggle helps us learn to deal with life and makes success possible, no matter what course we choose in life. To quote Spencer W. Kimball's life-long motto, "Just Do It."

※ ※ ※

Not so long ago on a reminiscent Christmas holiday to my aging parents Sacramento home, I took the time to visit the YMCA where I trained those many years before. I stood in front of those very same YMCA lockers. I sat on the very same bench remembering that moment in time, now more than a half century in the past.

Those early morning swim practices and the coach that ran them had long since passed away; this once beautiful facility had clearly served out its useful life. Nothing of that recent visit to the locker room was remotely as painful an experience as on that fateful day five decades earlier.

In those years I learned a lot about myself and in the ensuing decades those experiences lead to many wonderful opportunities. I had come full circle to arrive where I started. And although I had spent many hundreds of mornings in this locker room as a boy—now as I sat in contemplation I felt I knew this place for the very first time.

In my mind's eye, for just a moment, I thought perhaps I saw two young boys in a shadow of things that had been. The smaller of them sitting on that same bench with shoulders slumped just a little under the weight of his heavy burden of fears. The older boy after having stood by patiently, then sat down beside him.

How I well recalled our conversation that followed in that long ago moment in time; his promise still rings in my memory. There would be no retribution, no further suffering, no further humiliation for my act of sabotage. Instead there was a confident older boy telling a younger fearful, dejected, and lonely boy, "It will be all right. Everything will be okay."

The size of the Mad Dog's heart was not two sizes too small after all, and the release of tension from deep within my soul almost caused me to cry. But of course I couldn't—not there—not in front of him. Secretly, I had promised myself I would never tell anyone how kind and understanding he had been to me. That revelation, of course, would have caused irreparable damage to the Mad Dog's reputation. Then the shadows of the two boys disappeared through that door leading to the pool, as they walked out . . . together.

As the shadowy image of that fateful day further crystallized in my mind, I couldn't help but call out. "Don't you give up, boy. Don't you quit. Don't lose heart or your faith in mankind. You keep on going. You keep on trying. You keep on persevering one day at a time. I promise you there will be more help and happiness to come, a lot of it—fifty-four years of it now and still it's coming. You stand up for yourself with confidence and face your fears head-on. With your hand in the hand of Christ confront the challenges that life throws in your path. Push through those difficult days. It's all worth it. It will be all right in the end."[4]

✳ ✳ ✳

There is an epilogue to this story: On that long ago day I learned a valuable lesson that has served me well all the days of my life: sometimes we learn more from our failures in life than we do from our successes; and people are not always who they seem. The reputations for both our villains and our idols in life are often irrational, often based on an illusion derived from our fears and even more often far from the truth.

In fact John "Mad Dog" Fausnaut and I went on to become very good friends indeed. He was a warm, considerate, loyal friend, who helped to open my eyes, and let the future in. John went on to college on a football scholarship and I went on to college to swim and play water polo, where I learned about the gospel of Jesus Christ and to never again feel alone.

I met and later married the most beautiful Miss Anne Gray who has given me a wonderful life and four equally beautiful children, who have each married perfectly and have given us seven perfect grandchildren.

It could have all turned out differently, of course . . . but then, it didn't!

*Sadie had a warm and determined spirit that tugged at
Rachel's heartstrings the moment they met.*

# Rachel's Choice

Many years ago, when my children were young, they conspired against their dad to get a puppy. Despite the promises and indignant declarations to the contrary, I was certain that eventually the care and the inevitable puppy disasters would become the property of Mom and Dad. It was a blessing I felt certain I could do without. But Rachel, our eight-year-old, was unrelenting. Using her cutest little-girl charm, she did her very best to convince us all that was right, good, and praiseworthy in the world came from puppies.

One afternoon shortly after passing out my business cards to a boardroom full of chatty attorneys ready to begin their Christmas holiday, they each began to smirk and smile in that irritating way only attorneys can do. Written on the back of each business card was a separate and distinct appeal. Each read something like this: "My dad is mean. He won't let me get a puppy. Please talk him into it." They all seemed to revel in this unique and creative approach used by my daughter to sway the verdict. For the better part of half an hour I was harassed into surrender. This experience elevated my appreciation for the Lord's disdain of this particular profession, which led to our family proclamation: "If any of you children go to law school, you will be immediately disinherited."

Well, we arrived at Helen Woodward's dog rescue kennel early on a Saturday morning a week before Christmas. Cute little puppies of all shapes and sizes rushed us with hugs and kisses. But standing in their midst was one not-so-cute, scraggily, little mutt. A bit older than the rest, she had scarred, bowed legs with kneecaps that looked like baseball gloves. With big ears and the saddest little tail you have ever seen, she was unfashionably coarse with all the grace and elegance of a cinder block. But the final deterrent for so many potential owners, a long, ugly scar that ran down the center of her back. It was a sad reminder of another life that had not been so kind.

Rachel was the first to recognize Sadie's special quality. It seemed to overshadow her multitude of physical shortcomings. Sadie had a warm and determined heart that tugged at Rachel's heartstrings the moment they met. Rachel was insistent: "This is the one!" And soon the rest of our four children fell in line behind Rachel's choice.

My wife, Anne, informed the caretaker of our selection who in turn informed her, "Each member of your family must undergo a personal interview before taking Sadie home."

"Really? How ridiculous," I quietly whispered into Anne's ear when she shared the rescue kennel's demand with me. "We're not going to be interviewed to see if our family is suitable to take home some abandoned dog. We're the only ones who are willing to take this little mutt."

Anne stepped back and, with an unsettling, disturbing, irritated smile, let me know, "We will all be interviewing as a family, including you if necessary. You've agreed to get this dog, and your children want only this one, so prepare to smile and be pleasant!"

"Okay, Anne, okay. I get it," I said grudgingly. "But I can't do it this afternoon. I have a prior engagement."

"David," she said with a well-practiced, unnerving expression intended to paralyze its victim.

With a faltering confidence I meekly responded, "I promise, Anne, if after interviewing all of you they still want to talk to me, I will stop by Monday after work. I promise! Fair enough, my dear?"

Her only response was to put her hands on her hips and give me her patented sideways look designed to emasculate even the most confident husband, to make him wish he were back in the boardroom with that pack of rabid attorneys.

So an appointment was scheduled for later that day and Anne, my children, and the dog all eagerly attended. Rachel and her brothers were so excited. But, of course, after the interviews, Helen insisted I be interviewed as well. The family gathered in a united front and informed me that I really had no choice in the matter, but one: "Go to the interview."

"Okay," I conceded, "I will call and make arrangements to be there on Monday."

"No need. We already scheduled you for 5:30 today," Rachel said. "Don't mess this up, Dad!"

"Okay, Rachel, I'll be there," I said, laughing at her tenacity and the fact that she was probably a better negotiator at eight than I was at forty. Clearly, they had all joined forces to corner me, and there was little I could do to extricate myself. Checkmate—I was done for.

"Remember, David, this is very important to your children, especially Rachel," Anne reminded me before heading into the interview, as though I needed reminding. "So I want you to take this seriously."

I may have thought the interview requirement was ridiculous, but it was not as ridiculous as when Helen called Anne later that night to inform the family of her verdict. "Although you and your children passed with flying colors, unfortunately, your husband did not. I'm so sorry to tell you, but I am afraid we would not feel right releasing Sadie to a family who intends to keep her outside in a doghouse. For her well-being, she needs to be a part of the home, living inside with the family. I am so sorry, I know your children will be disappointed."

This summary judgment did not go down well with the family. I was threatened with immediate expulsion, and life as I had known it was over as far as my children were concerned. There were tears, anguish, and threats that no further chores would be done in the foreseeable future. To make things worse, I was dressed down with exceptional skill by a three-foot-tall, fire-breathing eight-year-old. "This was the perfect dog for our family, and you messed this up, Dad. I will never speak to you again for the rest of my entire life," Rachel wailed as if Armageddon had just arrived at our doorstep.

All of them looked at me as if I had brought the plague into our home and should be shunned and quarantined from their presence at all costs. It was difficult to admit, but in the short time my family had spent with Sadie, this determined, scruffy little dog with the ugly scar had overcome all her shortcomings and loved our family into submission. I was afraid that if it came down to me or Sadie, I was in trouble.

I swallowed my pride, called the Helen Woodward Kennel, and begged a follow up interview. She consented, and on the day before Christmas, I finally made it through the gauntlet of the Nuremburg Interrogation Trials on dog ownership. Of course I had to agree to certain concessions, signed in blood, including a home within our family home. Sadie would be a part of our family, or I might not be.

So on Christmas Eve, I clandestinely ushered Sadie into our little home, keeping her hidden in our bedroom all night until the next morning when Santa placed her under the tree with a beautiful red ribbon collar. As our four children all waited at the top of the stairs until the clock struck 6:00 a.m., the witching hour in our home, when all children and interested parties could come racing down the stairs to see what Santa, Grandma, Grandpa, or any other contributors might have put under the tree.

Of course Sadie couldn't wait that long. Her ears perked up. Her tail began wagging uncontrollably. Her scars clearly evident seemed to add to her cute, rascally, mischievous, irrepressible wriggling body. But it was her whimpering with delight for her new family when she heard our children at the top of the stairs that unleashed all self-control. Rachel burst through the barriers and down the stairs with her brothers right behind her to hug their new best friend, and Sadie squirmed free, racing to meet them at the bottom.

All was forgiven me. Or at least my transgressions were set aside as the joy of Christmas descended upon our family. Presents were few that morning, but all were happy, especially Rachel and Sadie. It was clear from the beginning that Christmas morning, Sadie would forever be a member of our family. With unyielding devotion to all of us, even me, Sadie carried that scar all the remainder of her life, but through the eyes of our family she was perfect in every way—our beautiful "Sadie Dog."

Many years later, when our children were all grown and most off on their own, we joined each other for what was to be Sadie's last Christmas. Her health was deteriorating quickly and yet her mind was still sharp. Her enthusiasm for life made us feel better as we sat around the Christmas tree. But her body could not keep up with her spirit. The usual signs of deafness and stiffness were clearly evident, and her legs would no longer carry her for those long runs in the park she had so loved. We knew we would need to make that difficult decision soon.

Anne had wrapped three of Sadie's favorite dog biscuits in red Christmas paper. She brought it out of the kitchen just as we finished unwrapping our last Christmas present and placed it in front of Sadie, who as always was laying in the midst of all the activity. "Now here you go Sadie, a present just for you!"

We cleared the floor of anything in her way and all made ready to watch her open her present. "Okay Sadie, its all yours," Mom further encouraged, as we all looked on like children in anticipation. She sniffed it and pawed it, then with one paw holding down her present Sadie pulled the paper loose with her teeth and other paw. We all smiled, and as always, Rachel encouraged her on. "You go, Sadie girl!"

For the next few minutes, Sadie opened and devoured her present, and all of us returned to those Christmases of many years ago when our children were young and the pure joy of sharing Christmas morning together as a loving family, laughing, cajoling, and smiling with each other. No matter what the passing of time brings, simple acts of heartfelt giving can reignite those feelings of love for one another in a family.

It wasn't but a few months later that Sadie passed away. We all gathered together in the backyard garden for her graveside funeral, each sharing personal stories of Sadie's inward beauty. All had tears in their eyes—including me.

＊＊＊

If we but pause for a moment, each of us can think of someone to whom life and the world has not been so kind; someone who may have been left with a scar or two, and yet rose above it, like our determined Sadie Dog with the scar on her back, that unusual someone with a beautiful heart and an indomitable spirit who has resolved to overcome their special challenges and make the best of life.

Frankly, I am humbled and inspired by so many in my circle of friends who have overcome varied and difficult challenges in their lives. They understand life doesn't always come tied with a red bow on Christmas morning, but still recognize it is an incredible gift from God nonetheless. They make the lives of those of us fortunate enough to be around them richer and more complete.

I recall the strong but humble man who was blinded and lost his family in a horrible accident as a young father, yet who each day reaches outside himself to be kind and cheerful to everyone he meets. Who with quick-witted humor reminds us, while there may be infectious disease and sorrow in the world, there is nothing so irresistibly contagious as laughter. He helps us all appreciate the everyday beauties of nature God has given us, to see with our eyes and to feel with our senses the beauty of the world around us.

I am reminded of a loving mother struck by a terrible incurable disease, who without complaint carries on with Christlike service to her family. She is an inspirational example to all mothers and fathers wherever they may be, whatever their circumstances. A daughter of the living God, she shares the beautiful blessings of the gospel with all she meets. She touches and inspires hearts with her humble sweetness and love.

And so, too, is another beautiful family with three almost-grown children who have adopted a severely handicapped child, a child who, like all of us, needs someone to love him. Watching this wonderful family care for Sam has been an inspiration and a blessing for the many in our congregation who have stepped up to share in the gospel blessing of serving one another, reaching out to take their turn at caring for Sam. What a wonderful legacy this family has brought to each of us in our congregation.

Each of our individual life stories are distinct and powerful in their own way, yet there is the common thread of the gospel of Christ that ties the fabric of our lives together. The world is filled with those who like Sadie have been scarred by life. The pity is, so many have not "discovered the healing balm of the Gospel of Christ to help them reap the blessings from overcoming these scars, to find true happiness, live life to its fullest and feel the comforting warmth that bathes the heart with peace and happiness as we serve each other."[1]

There are some who are young, trying to find themselves, determine who they are, what they can be, or even what they want to be. There are those who are afraid, but don't know of what. There are those who are angry, but don't know at whom. Those who want to be somebody and don't understand they already are in the eyes of God. Christ tells us if we but step outside ourselves and serve one another, we will find ourselves.

Others are in the midst of life, full of cares and worries that fill their days. Some allow their opinions or personal success to soar beyond their accomplishments inviting greed and envy to take their toll. Still others are stooped with age, burdened with care, or filled with doubt, living lives far below the level of their capacities. Yet all are children of our Heavenly Father who have much to offer if only the windows to their souls can be opened to the gospel of Jesus Christ. As Charles Dickens advised, "No space of regret can make amends for one life's opportunity missed."[2] For this purpose the Lord has provided "a marvelous work and a wonder," designed to "teach our *ears* to hear, our *eyes* to see, and our *hearts* to know the gospel of Jesus Christ, that He might heal us."[3]

What are the inspired ways of God? The counsel of Samuel the prophet echoes in our ears: "The Lord seeth not as man seeth; for man looketh on the outward appearance, but the Lord looketh on the heart."[4]

When the Savior needed a missionary of zeal and power, he found him not among his advocates, but in an adversary thought by most to be irretrievably scarred beyond redemption: Saul of Tarsus, a Sanhedrin Pharisee, Roman warrior, author of the warrant for the first Christian martyr, and dedicated to the destruction of the fledgling Christian Church. Saul breathed fear and trembling into every disciple of Christ, as he set out on the road to Damascus with death in his heart.

In Saul, Caiaphas the High Priest of the Sanhedrin had recognized the perfect instrument of terror to wipe out Christianity: a small, resolute, well-educated man seething with hate. Caiaphas had given him official letters, imprinted with his seal. It would open the doors to all of Judea to stamp out Christianity once and for all. How could Saul know that the road to Damascus would bisect his destiny and put him on a rendezvous with life itself?

Peter explained in awestruck wonder, "God is no respecter of persons." And again, "The Lord seeth not as man seeth." Of Saul the Lord declared: "He is a chosen vessel unto me to bear my name before Gentiles, kings, and the children of Israel: For I will show him how great he must suffer for my name's sake."[5]

As he drew near Damascus, tired, hungry, and covered with dust, Saul anticipated a good meal and the sweet night's rest at the inn on the "Street That Is Called Straight." Suddenly, there was a chill in the wind; he swayed in his saddle, a blinding light, and the roar of great waters in his ears. A moment later he lay on the ground, face in the dirt, helpless. He heard a voice strong, but compassionate, "Saul, Saul, why do you persecute me?"

Not daring to lift his face from the earth, Saul replied, "Lord, who are you?"

And the answer came in winning tones: "I am Jesus Christ, whom you persecute."

There could be no answer to that. Saul knew what these words meant, especially in relation to himself. Trembling with astonishment, Saul came to his knees, permanently blinded by the light; he faltered out the question that spelled his immediate, instantaneous, surrender: "Lord, what will you have me do?"[6]

He had left Jerusalem that morning seeing, but irrevocably scarred with a blindness to truth; he arrived in Damascus that evening blind, but for the first time in his life, "truly seeing" the gospel of Jesus Christ. Saul the persecutor became Paul the proselyter, Roman Citizen, and follower of Christ. "Born of water and the spirit, he could now enter the kingdom of God."[7]

Paul acknowledged his scars: "And lest I should be exalted above measure . . . there was given to me a thorn in the flesh . . . For this thing I sought the Lord. . . . And he said unto me, my grace is sufficient for thee; for my strength is made perfect in weakness."[8]

In this same letter to the Corinthians, the Apostle Paul taught: "God has chosen the weak things of the world to confound the mighty."[9] Paul was to dedicate the remainder of his life to the cause of truth. The Redeemer often chooses scarred and imperfect men to teach the way to perfection. He did so then. He does so now. Sometimes when we least expect it, the Lord chooses us, scarred individuals, to testify of the truthfulness of the Gospel of Jesus Christ to those who struggle to overcome their own scars in life.

We need no conflict of conscience. We need only the courage to stand with the Lord for our convictions. And in our struggle, should we stumble let us plead: "Lead us, oh great molder of men; out of the darkness to strive once again."[10] With Paul as our example, may we follow the Man from Galilee, overcome our scarred flaws, and so order our lives to reflect our love of Him.

"The voice of Christ comes ringing down through the halls of time asking each one of us, 'Do you love me?' And for every one of us, I answer as Luke did, 'Yea, Lord, we do love thee.' And having set our hand to the plough,' we will overcome our challenges and never look back until this monumental work is finished, and love of God and neighbor rules the world."[11]

Just as we loved our Sadie with the scar on her back, the Lord loves each of us despite our shortcomings, and with His healing balm lightens the burden of life's scars as we serve Him!

*I was much better suited for floating down the creek catching catfish, going frogging by the moonlight, or listening to Elvis sing about houndogs . . .*

# Christmas Traditions

*L*ike most boys growing up in the Heights, I was never one to allow schoolwork get in the way of my education. I made it a hard and fast rule to never take any schoolbooks home from Bell Avenue Elementary. Oh, I was willing to acknowledge that the preponderance of evidence did indeed suggest homework never killed no one. But the way I figured it, why take the chance? I conjectured, "Even if them schoolteachers was right and hard work paid off in time, why procrastination paid dividends in the right here and now." So when it came to schoolwork, I tried my best to follow the admonition of Mark Twain, "Never put off till tomorrow what you can do the day after tomorrow."[1]

The way I saw it, proper homework was making jumping ramps for our bikes, fishing rafts for the creek, or innovating prehistoric skateboards out of my sister's metal roller skates and some discarded two-by-fours. Frankly, my buddies and I could make just about anything from a few scraps from the lumber yard, four Red Ryder wagon wheels, or some equally valuable find from Mean Eddy's Junk-Yard down on the corner: go-carts, forts, or even fashioning a Gatling rubber-gun mounted on an old office swivel chair that could shoot in every direction. Of course some of the specialty items had to be acquired using the five-finger discount plan, on account of our lack of available financing.

Unlike the more obedient repentant boys, we sometimes played hooky to float down the creek catching catfish, going frogging by the moonlight, or listening to Elvis sing about hound dogs . . . and sometimes sneaking into the 49er drive-in to watch the likes of Ben Hur thrash the living daylights out of those Roman Legions.

I suppose some might say growing up in the Heights was like being banished to a cultural and spiritual wasteland. But then that's only the opinion of folks living on the right side of the tracks. My family saw life from an entirely different corner of the world, through the lens of our own peculiar brand of undiagnosed social disorders, abnormal behaviors, and personality neuroses.

A cultural event in our family was getting up early Sunday morning, hopping on a bus with rich Uncle Joey, lunch bag in tow, to take in a ball game down at Candle Stick Park. As dad put it, "Heaven on earth is watching the San Francisco Giants playing the LA Dodgers on a Sunday afternoon with peanuts and Cracker Jacks; Sandy Koufax on the mound facing Willie Mays at the plate with the game on the line. A spiritual experience like no other, with a cheering crowd that could make the earth move under your feet."

The only unpardonable sins in our family: paying retail, or worse, missing a K-Mart "Blue Light Special." In fact, I'm told my very first spoken words were, "Attention K-Mart shoppers."

Sure we had our traditions. Every year on Thanksgiving weekend, on our way home from the Flyshaker Pool Swim Meet in San Francisco, we'd stop off at the Chuck-A-Rama buffet for Thanksgiving dinner, affectionately known in our neighborhood as the Up-Chuck-A-Rama. My favorite, the "Artery Clogger"—two pigs wrapped in a blanket, deep fried onion rings smothered in good old American Cheese Whip, and a marshmallow shake covered in whip cream with a maraschino cherry on top, guaranteed to be made up of at least 50 percent cancer-causing agents. And on Christmas Day, we added a quarter of an apple pie a la mode.

While most folks start their Christmas shopping around Halloween, our family waited till Christmas Eve when you could get a K-Mart tree for free, Santa's presents on the cheap, and a boatload of silver tinsel for next to nothing.

We set up the Christmas tree in the middle of our living room floor, stood in a circle around it, then flung on the shiny silver tinsel till it looked like a silver missile heading to the moon. Then we'd leave it there until March, hoping no one dropped a match. And Christmas lights, well, they could still be hanging from the rafters as far as I know.

❄ ❄ ❄

No one in my neighborhood had even stepped foot on a college campus, except maybe to cut off the head of a parking meter for the dimes. And any discussion with my neighborhood buddies on goal-setting or inspirational accomplishments invariably began with some perceptively insightful comment like: "Come in here, Corkey, and take a look at this-un, afore I flush it down."

Frankly, I wasn't sure our family gene pool even had a deep end. So when I was offered scholarships to swim and play water polo in college, it was more than a seminal event in my life. It opened up a whole new world for me.

I stepped onto campus, knowing virtually nothing of college life and even less of the institution that sponsored it. That's when I met my very first college friend who was also a member of this church. Ray took me to see The Choir in Concert. To say I was impressed would be a cataclysmic understatement and a colossal underestimation of the impact on my life.

In our home, classical music was the National Anthem where the last line always ended in "play ball," or Country Joe and the Fish singing, "I Feel Like I'm Fixin' To." The only Mozart I knew was Eddy Mozart, whose old man owned the junkyard down on the corner.

Even now when I am probably the only member of our church asked to never join the congregational choir, I clearly recall being left with a feeling of awe for the beauty, majesty, and emotional power of the music performed by The Choir those many decades ago. It brought the first glimpse of the powerful impact the gospel of Christ was to have on my life.

It was on campus where I first met the fetching Anne Gray, born across the pond in England, the epicenter of all culinary and cultural life. And after a year of dinners, the likes of which I could never even have imagined, it was clear Chuck-A-Rama had lost its savor and Anne Gray had won my heart.

Then of course, came talk of marriage, as was customary on campus. In fact marriage was such an avid preoccupation with so many students, I naturally assumed the message was clear: marriage would bring an end to all troubles. I didn't realize it was the front-end they were talking about.

Eager to discuss wedding plans, my mom, dressed in far less than her bare essentials, received my future mother-in-law Beryl Gray at the front door of our little home. Speechless and flustered, Beryl, the epitome of etiquette on everything proper and culturally efficacious, just couldn't find the words to return the welcome. But it was mom's welcoming hug in her birthday suit that really broke the ice.

To say ours was a clash of cultures would be a blatant insult to the term "understatement." My whole world was turned upside down. Anne read Dickens, studied Beethoven, and it was clear from the beginning my family traditions would never leave the bullpen.

Anne brought to our new family a culture that had been forged through centuries of English heritage and refined in the cauldron fire of centuries of religious tradition. She even knew which fork to use at the Christmas dinner table. Have you ever seen someone eat their peas with a knife and fork? Well, I won't go there. Let's just say there would be no more Christmas trees that looked like a silver missile heading to the moon.

Thanksgiving in our little home conjured up images of Pilgrims landing at Plymouth Rock, with sumptuous feasts the likes of which my family growing up could never even have imagined. And a month before Santa came down the chimney, our home was infused with the spirit of Christmas—a wonderful and curious mix of the Little Town of Bethlehem, Canterbury Tales, and Santa's Village all rolled into one,

*Anne even knew which fork to use at the Christmas dinner table.*

eventually with little elves of our own under foot to join in the celebration. Our new family traditions were the envy of the block, and I fell in love all over again.

One of our favorite Christmas traditions is Charles Dickens's *A Christmas Carol*. The 1951 version with Alistair Sims as Scrooge is the best. We all know the story. My favorite scene is Ebenezer Scrooge, having spent a miserable Christmas dinner accompanied solely by himself at the local pub. He settles down in front of the fire in his cold, dingy, uninviting house. All alone, with a blanket wrapped around him to save money on coal. He hears a knock at the door. A bit nervous and annoyed, he snuggles deeper into his big chair only to be interrupted yet again with another, even harder knock at the door. This time in comes old Jacob Marley, his ex-partner who unfortunately has been dead for the past seven Christmases.

A conversation ensues. Ebenezer, bewildered, perturbed, and just a little afraid, blusters his way through the exchange insisting that Jacob is just a figment of his imagination. "Probably an undigested bit of potato," as he puts it. After all Jacob is dead, isn't he? Scrooge attempts to ignore Jacobs's efforts to explain the long, ponderous chain he drags behind him. Nevertheless, Jacob persists, explaining that it had been forged in life by his own selfish choices.

Ebenezer Scrooge to Jacob Marley, "You were just a good man of business." To which Jacob, enraged, rattles his chains to terrorize Ebenezer and replies in an agonizing voice of frustration, "Business? Mankind was my business." And so the story goes, Ebenezer Scrooge is terrified and, before going to sleep that night, checks under his bed for Christmas, only to find himself and the gospel of Jesus Christ. In the end Scrooge acknowledges Christ's Christmas message, "Love thy neighbor as thyself"[2] and "As I have loved you . . . love one another."[3]

*✳ ✳ ✳*

Some years ago while in London on business, I had the opportunity to visit the office of the long since passed away British Barrister, "Ebenezer Scrooge," who had inspired this wonderful tale. This attorney had put Charles Dickens's father into debtor's prison a decade before Dickens wrote *A Christmas Carol*.

It was sobering to stand in front of that office and contemplate the legacy left to the world by this man. A life yielded to selfish passions, selfish hopes, and selfish desires only to be lost to the sorrow and misery of his unfortunate victims. He let his own selfishness get in the way of what matters most in life.

Thomas S. Monson so eloquently advises, "Stresses in our lives come regardless of our circumstances. We must deal with them the best we can: But we should not let them get in the way of what is most important—and what is most important almost always involves the people around us. Often we assume that they must know how much we love them. But we should never assume. . . . We will never regret kind words spoken, or the affection shown. . . . Never let a problem to be solved become more important than a person to be loved. . . . This is our one and only chance at mortal life—here and now. The longer we live, the greater is our realization that it is brief. Opportunities come, and then they are gone."[4]

One of the greatest lessons learned is the art of distinguishing between what is important for our family, friends, those around us, and what is not. Choose your loves in life wisely, then live your choices completely. Do not let those most important things pass you by as you plan for that elusive, nonexistent future when you will be able to do what you want, when you want to do it.

Don't be the one who learns too late, most important of all life blessings is the love of your wife, the love of your children, the warmth of a family, the companionship of a friend, the lift in your step when you've done something for someone else, and the recognition of the comforting spirit of Christ in your life. Grab those opportunities when they come your way. Don't wait for the future. Revel in these things, here and now. "You pile up enough tomorrows, and you'll find you've collected a lot of empty yesterdays."[5]

"Near the end of his life, one father looked back on how he had spent his time on earth. An acclaimed, respected author of numerous scholarly works, he said, 'I wish I had written one less book and taken my children fishing more often.' Time passes quickly."[6] It seems like yesterday that I left my neighborhood behind never to return; married the fetching Anne Gray; witnessed my children being born into this world. Now those children are grown with children of their own. Where did the years go?

We cannot call back time once it has passed; we cannot stop the present from coming; we cannot experience the future before it arrives. Time is a gift. It is a treasure that cannot be put aside for the future. Instead, time should be used wisely in the present to establish well those family traditions and strengthen family ties for eternity.

God bless you all, and may you all have a Merry Christmas!

*A call to serve; the Christmas gift that would change their lives forever!*

# His Christmas Gift

Children in the home at Christmas time are always a blessing. They bring to life the spirit of Christmas. But we seldom expect our children will take this opportunity to impart life-changing wisdom into our lives. Yet sometimes it is a child whom can best teach us the most valuable lessons of life. May I acquaint you with a story of a son, who inspired his parents to an unexpected understanding of the scripture "whereas I was blind, now I see."[1]

Nineteen-year-old Jeff, home from college for Christmas, delivered a gift to his parents they had certainly not expected and were entirely unprepared to receive. Jeff informed them he would not be returning to college next semester, but instead serving a two-year mission for his church. In fact arrangements had already been made.

Jim and Jody sat stunned, bewildered and distraught after Jeff opened his mission call. It was certainly not the Christmas present they had hoped for. Jody, in tears, was having none of it. "This is my boy; he is too young to be traveling to some far away dangerous corner of the world, to live with people I have never even met," she said in a letter to Gordon B. Hinckley, the President of The Church of Jesus Christ of Latter-day Saints at the time.

These wonderful parents had thought this church was just another passing adolescent fancy like skateboards, surfing, or baseball. Now they knew differently. President Hinckley, poignantly touched by this dedicated and sweet mother's defense of her son, wanted only the best for this family. In the hope their hearts might be softened, he asked Thomas S. Monson if he might call upon Jody and Jim, then follow up with President Christopher Waddell.

"We are not human beings having a spiritual experience; we are spiritual beings having a human experience."[2] We are all children of our Father in Heaven looking for the light of Christ to illuminate an ever-darkening world. Through thoughtful prayer, President Hinckley revised the call to Preston, England. This was the mission that had made such a difference in President Hinckley's life; he hoped it would do the same in the lives of this wonderful family. After four months of gentle persuasion, Jim and Jody resigned themselves, Jeff would be leaving on a two-year mission for his church.

❋ ❋ ❋

Jeff stood at the pulpit for his missionary farewell; Jim and Jody sat front and center, right below the podium. Both were mystified by their son's remarkable, seemingly unyielding commitment to this church and his insistence on leaving everything behind for a mission to a foreign land. Jody had broken down in tears when she realized her son would be two continents away, and she couldn't visit or even speak to him but twice a year. His father, Jim, in church for the very first time, arms folded, jaw set and eyebrows furled, sat in stone-cold silence staring straight ahead.

Many sat in the congregation, hoping and praying that Father in Heaven might ease the obvious concern in the eyes of these two dedicated parents. Many knew them both and longed to have the Spirit touch their hearts and ease their pain as Jeff stood at the pulpit.

Jeff's concerned countenance transformed into contagious excitement as he began to speak. With a warm inviting sparkle in his eye, an infectious smile began to spread wide across his face. The exuberant enthusiasm in Jeff's manner immediately engaged the congregation. This little surfer boy spoke to a full house. "I'm gonna miss my bros, my mom and dad, and all of you," he said, "but it's gonna be totally awesome hookin' up with all those cool English dudes. I'm totally stoked!"

And so it began. Jeff left for his mission amid tears from Mom and a stern resolute commitment from Dad to separate myth from the truth of this church. Week after week they came to sacrament meeting, not to learn about the gospel, but to understand the motive behind their son and to uncover the clandestine intensions of this church. At first they sat by themselves. But then a marvelous thing happened as Bishop Crickmore, the Gwilliams, the Eks, the Berthas, and others in the congregation reached out to them, and letters flowed in from their son. The Spirit of the Lord touched their hearts and they began to glimpse His "Plan of

Happiness." The gospel of Christ slowly seeped into their very souls and before they recognized what was happening, Jody and Jim Yates found themselves among the converted.

The weeks rolled into months and on Christmas Day the following year, Jeff spoke to his parents for the very first time. This wonderful family shared the deepest thoughts of their heart over a six thousand mile phone line. Tears of joy were shed as they each spoke of the transformation in their lives. The Spirit was in the air as Jim bore testimony to his son of Christ's church here on this earth, sealed with the blood of a prophet. They agreed right then and there—Jeff would baptize them both when he returned from his mission.

But the congregation had other ideas. Jeff's mission president was contacted, arrangements made, and Bishop Crickmore handed them two plane tickets to London, England, purchased by a caring member of the congregation. Jim and Jody would be flying to England to be baptized by their son.

Jeff and the little congregation where he had been serving for several months were informed. They could hardly contain their excitement. Final preparations were made for the upcoming baptism. Then just before the big event, as his parents made final preparations for the trip, Jeff's mission president informed him, "You are being transferred to another part of the mission. I'm sorry, Jeff. I know it's unexpected, but it comes direct from your Father in Heaven. I don't know why, but I have learned to listen to the Spirit when inspired."

Neal Maxwell, a General Authority of the Church, has said: "The youth of this generation have a greater capacity for obedience than any other previous generation."[3] That night Jeff knelt in prayer, poured out his heart to his Father in Heaven and the warm, comforting Spirit of the Lord brought peace to his soul; inspired by the scripture, "Be still, and know that I am God,"[4] and all will be well.

The following day, Jeff was in his new congregation and a guest for dinner with the Preston family. Jeff shared the unsettling story of the pending baptism scheduled for the following Saturday, then the surprising transfer. Quiet settled over the room as the realization that the family of Stephanie Gwilliam, who had played such an instrumental role in Jeff's conversion as well as that of his parents six thousand miles away in California, had once been a cornerstone of this very congregation decades before. In fact, President Preston, the new Ashton, England stake president had been Stephanie's best friend growing up, spending much of his formative youth in her childhood home. But then Stephanie's family had immigrated to America.

Calls were made, arrangements finalized, and on a beautiful spring day in Preston, England, Jeff baptized his parents with both congregations in attendance. Even their Cardiff Church family from across the pond in America participated. The entire Cardiff Church had secretly pre-recorded a baptismal segment just for the occasion. All joined in singing "I Am a Child of God." Tears were shed by many that day, friendships from across the Atlantic were rekindled, and the gospel of Christ claimed yet another family. The caring friend who had brought them to England introduced them to the Preston, England temple president who set the wheels turning for their family to be sealed together in the temple.

The following year, Jeff once again stood at the same podium where he had given his farewell two years before. This time it was for his homecoming. With compelling conviction he shared a very personal, stirring, and powerful testimony in perfect King's English. Mom and Dad sat speechless as they witnessed the transformation of this wonderful young man. This time tears of happiness streamed down both their faces.

"We laughed. We cried. We were astonished as Jeff inspired and held the entire congregation transfixed," Jim was to later say.

Jeff quoted Winston Churchill from memory, who half a century earlier, spoke to the world at war, "Do not let us speak of darker days; let us rather speak of sterner days. These are not dark days; these are great days. The greatest days our Country has ever lived; and we must all thank God that we have been allowed, each of us according to our stations, to play our part in making these days memorable in the history of all mankind."

Those in attendance will never forget the transformed presence of this young man and his very powerful testimony. Shortly thereafter, Jim and Jody Yates knelt across the altar of the temple, to be sealed to each other. With tears of happiness streaming down both their faces, they were then sealed to their son Jeff for time and all eternity. At that moment they knew in their hearts the Christmas gift received almost three years before had been the greatest gift of their lives. They now knew what real joy and happiness felt like. They knew what their Savior meant when he said, "I am the light of the world: he that followeth me shall not walk in darkness, but shall have the light of life."[5] For they had been blinded by the darkness of the unknown, but now they saw through the light of Christ. For the light of Christ illuminated the full blessing of His Christmas gift.

*But for the intervention of those in the lifeboat willing to risk their own lives for another, the human tragedy was inevitable.*

# A Christmas for Sadie

While working in London some years ago, I had the opportunity to visit the Victoria & Albert Museum. There were many wonderful masterpieces by artists who throughout the centuries depicted scenes from life and times long since past. The very best masters elicited emotions from deep within the viewer who gazed into the artistic portrayal of the human experience.

One particular masterpiece reflected an interpretation of the age-old life struggle of man against the sea. The intriguing masterpiece painted by Joseph Turner in 1831, entitled "To the Rescue," depicts unsettling, ominous, black clouds filling tumultuous skies. Furious driving wind and torrential rainfall toss a struggling vessel about in a turbulent sea of powerful, angry waves.

The painting foreshadows danger and even death to a seemingly hapless vessel fighting for life as it struggles to avoid being thrown onto the rocks. It conveys to the viewer the emotions of panic, moral courage, and compassion for another human, which only the very best masters of the centuries old craft can evoke from their art.

A bright light gleaming off the vessel through the angry night make it possible for a wife and two small children standing on the shore to watch the tragedy unfold before their very eyes. Wet and whipped by wind, the frantic, helpless mother and children gaze anxiously out to sea toward their fishermen in peril.

In the foreground of the painting, between the vessel and the distraught family members on the beach is a lifeboat being tossed about in the foaming waves of the tempest. The hapless souls in the lifeboat pull desperately on the oars, braving the turbulent seas to come to the rescue of the fishermen.

The scene portends the human tragedy about to unfold, but for the intervention of the poorly equipped few who are willing to risk their own lives to rescue their fellowmen. As the scripture says, "Greater love hath no man than this, that a man lay down his life for his friends."[1]

* * *

Amid the storms of life, danger lurks for all of us from time to time, for that is the nature Earth. Here is where our Father in Heaven has placed us to struggle against obstacles of life, that we might grow closer to Him from the experience.

Each of us at times find ourselves stranded, facing danger, heartache, or distress. Maybe not this time or even the next, but at one time or another we will face the rocks on a stormy night. Who will man the lifeboat? Who will leave behind the familiar comforts of home and family and go out into the stormy night to help with the rescue in those, our inevitable times of need? Who will follow the admonition of Christ, "Thou shalt love thy neighbor as thyself"[2]?

Will you and I be held responsible for those we might have helped or even saved, had we softened our heart and stepped up to do our duty for those friends and neighbors around us in their time of need, to help with our Father in Heaven's work wherever we can? Ours is the privilege to be not spectators, but participants on the stage of life; to recognize and act upon opportunities; to lend a helping hand to our neighbors when needed. "If we don't try, we don't do; and if we don't do, then why are we here?"[3] As Christ reminds us, "When ye are in the service of your fellow beings ye are only in the service of your God."[4]

* * *

Some years ago, on a Thanksgiving Day, during an especially difficult financial climate in our country, I had occasion to speak to our neighbor, Melissa, a wonderful and loving mother of four beautiful young children. Melissa is blessed with a heart of gold and a loving husband, who despite his best efforts found himself unemployed during this dark downturn in our economy. Like many during that period, David had been out of work for some time, but was doing his best to find part-time work and provide for his loving family. David and Melissa counted every penny just to put food on the table for a family of six and keep the creditors away from their home tightly packed with children and love.

Earlier that Thanksgiving day, Melissa had received a call from a county social worker informing her that her fourteen-year-old niece, Sadie, had just lost yet another foster home and had no place to spend the Thanksgiving holiday. The social worker wondered if Melissa and her family might be able to accommodate Sadie for a time.

Melissa followed the admonition of the Apostle Paul, and she was an example of her religion. She holds the spirit of Christ close to her heart, always willing to reach out and help. In her sweet and caring way, Melissa agreed. "Of course I will, at least for the holiday." But because of the lack of room in her already cramped home and her family's financial struggles, she let the social worker know it could only be temporary.

As she related this to me, I could see how much this wonderful mother struggled and grieved for her niece. A tear came to her eye as she told the story of Sadie's alcoholic father, long since absent mother, and the heartache this young girl was undergoing after losing yet another temporary home. "If only we had the room in our house, but it's already bursting at the seams," she shared with a tear. "If we could just squeeze her in, we would find a way to make it work. We could stretch a dollar just a little further. After all, how much can she really cost us? I'm sure we can feed one more. If only we could find a way to squeeze three into one of these bedrooms." Here was love in action. Here was an unspoken sermon of caring.

I knew all would be well with Sadie if Melissa could find a way to take her in. For Melissa understood family is a refuge of safety from the stormy seas of life. Her home is a portage of peace, where she and her husband loved, comforted, and cared for their gifts from heaven and taught the essential truths of life, faith, hope, and charity. Both David and Melissa were ready, willing, and engaged with their family, instilling God-given commitments that transcend personal desires and aspirations. I was certain Melissa and David would bring Sadie into their circle of love, if only given the opportunity.

❋ ❋ ❋

All of our children remember the home of their childhood. Their thoughts do not dwell on whether our home was stylish or not, big or not, our neighborhood upscale or not. Rather, they delight in the experiences we shared as a family. Our home was the laboratory of their lives. What they learned at home, for good or bad, largely determined who they were when they left us.

There were years while our children were little, when we found it difficult to see through the misty clouds of the future to that day when they might stand on their own—as loving, caring, responsible grown-ups. Then one day they were there—it's a beautiful thing for a parent to watch.

Thanksgiving dinner was one of those times in our lives when Anne and I felt the full gratitude of being blessed with wonderful children. I asked the question of my now grown children and their spouses: "Would you be willing to forego your own Christmas plans to instead build a bedroom for Sadie and this deserving family—our treasured neighbors?" All were extremely busy with the hustle and bustle of life, pursuing their careers, aspirations, and other interests in life. All had lives packed full of obligations. Nevertheless, without exception, each volunteered to set aside their own personal Christmas plans to help Sadie settle into a home with Melissa, David, and their caring family. All agreed to offer to build a bedroom for Sadie and her new family. It would be our Christmas present to them and to each other. My children and their spouses began planning even before I had an opportunity to ask the question of Melissa. Sleep was slow in coming that night. I was excited for the morning to come and the opportunity to make the proposal. To make David and Melissa an offer they couldn't refuse.

The following day, I met with Melissa and David to ask if we might build a bedroom addition on their home. They were both surprised and thankful for the offer, but couldn't imagine how they could possibly afford it.

"No, it's just not possible," was their answer.

I let them know it would be a favor from our family. We were interested only in the opportunity to reach out to such a deserving family as theirs who were willing to embrace the enormous task of taking in Sadie, with four children already and a difficult financial situation.

"It's your decision of course, but please know we will be disappointed if we can't help," I said. "You have my promise, if you do decide to allow it, we will build the bedroom for a price you can't refuse."

With tears in their eyes, both let us know this was an answer to their prayers. Melissa and David agreed to take the risk, to trust us; to allow our family to help theirs.

We were on our way. Although David and Melissa didn't quite know what to think. And secretly, they had their fingers crossed, hoping we wouldn't mess it up.

For the next three weeks, we got to work. The entire family joined in the project. We quickly put together a redesign of a portion of their garage to add a fully furnished bedroom for Sadie.

Our daughter Rachel and her husband Jason, the MacGyvers of our family, were the first to volunteer building materials—lumber, electrical supplies, and hardware.

Paul and a pregnant Elizabeth helped acquire the drywall, tape, and mud.

Michael provided the carpet and padding, and Daniel promised to help with labor over his Christmas break.

All of us worked together, putting in time after work, on weekends, or whenever we could find a moment. We marked out the bedroom, leveled in a subfloor, built walls, pulled electrical, installed outlets, windows, and doors, and hung drywall.

Then in a minor miracle, Sadie's father volunteered to tape, mud, and finish the walls and ceiling. When he finished, his eyes filled with tears, and his emotion touched our hearts.

Melissa and David were so appreciative. Their wonderful children brought us lemonade and sandwiches. They joined in the work and the laughter—a lot of laughter. Christ's touch and influence was recognizable in their lives. They had been taught to love and serve one another. What a beautiful family. We weren't just adding to a house built of lumber, drywall, and carpet. In our small way, we were helping to add to a home made of love, sacrifice, and respect; a safe portage for a young girl from the tempests and storms of life; and a unique and lasting relationship between two families. A home can become a heaven on earth when it shelters a family using a blueprint drawn by the master architect of our lives.

The days passed and work progressed. We finished painting two days before Christmas. Then our good friend Kevin helped us install the carpet.

Finally the room was finished as darkness fell on Christmas Eve, then furnished with dresser, bed, end tables, and lighting. It was a beautiful sight and all our hearts were filled with the Christmas spirit, an increased understanding of one another and a caring that brought us all closer through the experience. Hugs were shared all around and even a tear or two shed between friends and family, with a card wishing a Merry Christmas, "a gift from our family to yours."

As the lingering remnants of our family walked out into the night air and down the block to our home on that Christmas Eve, each of us felt the spirit of Christmas. Not a word was spoken; we were tired, but felt the warmth of Christ in our hearts. As Christ encouraged, by love we had served one another. It was indeed a labor of love from all concerned, drawing both families together and establishing a special bond with Sadie that would never be broken. The line between giver and receiver became blurred over those three weeks.

There were no Christmas presents under the tree in our home that year, but there was a warm comforting feeling of the Christmas spirit in our hearts. The Spirit of Christ was evident in our family as we shared our Christmas dinner together. We knew we had done as our Savior asked. We had shown love to our neighbor, and it felt good.

✳ ✳ ✳

"Home is where the heart is." Our home and families fashion our beliefs in preparation for the rest of our lives. These are the building blocks of society. We must build our homes wisely because eternity is not a short voyage. There will be calm days and stormy ones, sunny afternoons and dark nights, the joy of bringing loved ones together and the sorrow of watching them pass away. But if we do it right, our home and memories of family can be a bit of heaven on earth.

A Merry Christmas and God bless us all, everyone!

*"The act of a special love passing between father and son on a Christmas Day . . . a feeling difficult to describe, but impossible to forget."*

# Never a Finer Christmas

*C*hristmas morning 1958, I was eight years old. Like most boys growing up in the 1950s, my passion in life was for that great American pastime—baseball. America was in the midst of baseball's Golden Age: Willie Mays, Ted Williams, Satchel Paige, and Joltin' Joe DiMaggio. These were the idols of young boys in struggling neighborhoods all across the country.

Any time I could spend with my buddies playing baseball in the alleyway, away from the harsh realities of the barrio, was time prized above all else in life. We had a couple of big old wooden bats with cracked handles and a half dozen baseballs that had long since lost their leather covers, hand-me-downs from my dad. There was never a broken bat or coverless ball that couldn't be fixed with a couple of Dixie Line screws and a little tape. We never threw 'em away—just wore 'em out!

Wrapped and rewrapped with black electrical tape, the baseball picked up small pebbles and bits of broken glass from the concrete alleyway. There was many a time I squeezed back tears after taking Leron Lee's notorious "Midnight Rider" fastball in on the hands. Some said Leron threw so hard, he could throw a lamb chop right past a coyote. And he hit the ball so far, on one occasion it didn't come down from the sky until we all came back to play the next day, when Slick Sweezy caught it in centerfield and the ump called Leron out for the game from the day before.

Standing just outside the batter's box, I'd jangle it around kinda gently like. You know, to keep them juices flowing, like we'd seen them do down at Candlestick Park, where the San Francisco Giants had just opened a franchise. I'd choke halfway up the handle of that big old bat just so I could swing it, then step up to the plate to take care of business.

I could drive a baseball on a line like a rocket. Unfortunately, sometimes it rocketed right down the alleyway and through the front window of Old Mrs. Bliss's rickety ramshackle house. Her broken window was considered a ground-rule home run, but of course, we'd scatter like cockroaches in mom's kitchen when she turned on the light 'cause that old lady was without a doubt the meanest old woman God ever blew breath into.

Dad, who was the final answer to all disputes on our block, would insist I apologize and pay penance for my indiscretion. With my head hung down humble like, hat in hand, I'd ask for forgiveness from the old lady while she twisted my ear and gave me "the what for," and her dog Boots gave me the evil eye. There were many occasions when that flea-bitten little mutt chased me down to bite my butt something awful. I was afraid of that mangy little dog until long after he was too old to chase me down, and I was too old to admit it.

Dad would apologetically replace the window glass and I'd pay penance for my transgression by push mowing her lawn and trimming the plants. I spent a lot of hours working in that yard and kept it looking pretty nice too, if I do say so myself. You might say my breaking her window glass on a regular basis was kind of a gift to old Mrs. Bliss. Hers was the only lawn on our block and she clung to it like it was her sole link to the sane world.

❄ ❄ ❄

I cherished my Christmas vacation like no other. But that particular year was different. Each morning I rolled out of bed at seven and gathered with my buddies at the open field behind Eddie Mozart's junkyard to pull weeds, dig up rocks, and grade a ball field for the big game on Christmas Day. We finished our grading and smoothing on Christmas Eve, completing the final touches by nailing down wooden blocks for bases, lining it with chalk from the junkyard, then we sat back in solemn appreciation of our efforts. It was an inspiring sight! All our dads, or their stand-ins, said it was the finest ball field they'd ever seen, then committed right then and there to play in the big game on Christmas Day. Which didn't happen often frankly, never as far as I can recall. They were just too busy workin', drinkin', or boxin' our ears every other day of the year.

We had some pretty interesting dads too. Bug's stepdad was a real live Apache, who was built like a beer keg and certainly not unfamiliar with its contents either. Sweezy's mom's boyfriend drove an awesome-cool garbage truck, had arms like jackhammers from lifting trash cans all day, with plenty of tattoos to celebrate Rosie the Riveter and other ladies. Both Leron's and Artist's dads had played baseball in the Negro Leagues. But all agreed, without a doubt I was the luckiest kid they knew, on account of my dad's celebrity status. He had returned from fighting in the Big War to play minor league baseball in the Pacific Coast League for the San Francisco Seals. Because of it, my buddies looked on me with a certain reverent envy. There was no question about it—our First Annual Christmas Day Ballgame would be the biggest game of the century.

Like all boys, Christmas was a big day for me. I awoke that Christmas morning in 1958 thinking not about gifts under the tree, but rather about the Christmas ballgame to be played later that afternoon with all my buddies, their dads, stepdads, or significant other stand ins. Nevertheless to my everlasting surprise, Santa brought me PF Flyers that Christmas: the only tennis shoe guaranteed to make you run faster and jump higher.

❈ ❈ ❈

I stepped onto the ball field that Christmas afternoon in my Flyers, with my glove on my left hand, my bat in my right ready and as excited as excited can be to play in the big game. That's when Dad reached into his back pocket and pulled out a brand spanking new, official Pacific Coast League professional baseball. He tossed it to me and said, "Here you go, son. It's for the game." Then he put his arm around my shoulder and walked me onto the field for all to see.

A rush of unadulterated pride poured into my very soul. I thought my chest was going to burst as my buddies Corkey, Bug, Leron, Artist, Buttlicker, and Sweezy looked on me with unabashed adulation.

It wasn't that the ball was expensive; it probably cost only a couple of quarters. But this act of humanity, of kindness, and consideration so uncommon in our world, touched my heart and near brought me to tears. This reflection of a special love passing between a father and son would make this Christmas one I would never forget. For in that moment time stood still. There seemed only my father and me, standing all alone, above the harsh realities of our troubled neighborhood. It gave me a feeling difficult to describe, but impossible to forget as the spirit of Christmas seeped deep into my heart.

The riches of the game of baseball are in the thrills and moments of near exaltation, and we had plenty of them that Christmas day. We played our brand of raucous baseball all afternoon and into the evening twilight until that ball was scuffed and worn. Then we all walked home together, as fathers and sons—talkin' baseball. My dad had played like Mays, the Splendid Splinter and old Joltin' Joe, all wrapped up in one. Of course, us boys bragged-up our exploits on the ball field that day, talking smack and dancing around like nobody was a watching.

We decided right then and there how we were going to do it all again next year, and every year there after. But for the life of me, I don't recall it ever happing anything like that day ever again. Days like that one are here, and then they're gone. There was never a finer Christmas! For on that day, I knew there was not a boy any place in this whole wide world who had a more awesome dad than mine!

✳ ✳ ✳

Ralph Waldo Emerson wrote, "Rings and jewels are not gifts, but apologies for gifts. The only gift is a of thyself."[1] The miracle of Christmas is seldom found in the excess of things. It is less obvious upon arrival, and more lasting in its impact. It is often in the simple moments that touch our hearts and change our lives. The moments that bring to our impressionable hearts a warmth having little to do with worldly goods, but a whole lot to do with family relationships, with time together sharing our passions and love for one another, with patience, with compassion and caring.

As a boy I saw my father as an infallible anchor to my reality and truth. But as time passed, the simple clarity of my childhood faded and the luster of my heroes tarnished, including my admiration for my father. I began to take for granted those moments in my life that most deserved my gratitude, the very people who most deserve my appreciation. Regardless of our circumstances, the turmoil in our world, the difficult problems we face, every one of us has much to be grateful for if we but pause and contemplate our blessings.

I don't remember exactly when it happened, but the simplicity of my boyhood outlook on life vanished. And sometime in my adolescent youth, my father's blemishes became apparent and my image of him as my hero unraveled. I recognized he was indeed fallible, that his judgment was not always wise, his thinking true, or his sentences just. He was indeed just like the rest of us, a simple fallen man.

Disappointed, in time I arrogantly resented him for his imperfections, as is often the case with a teenager's self-centered outlook on life. I saw only his flaws glaring back at me. I forgot my many blessings and instead dwelt upon my misfortune.

As my world expanded into other neighborhoods, I thought myself disadvantaged, cheated by my upbringing, embarrassed by where I came from. I was reluctant to take my new friends home to meet my family. The Greek philosopher Epictetus tells us, "He is a wise man who does not grieve for things which he has not, but rejoices for those which he has." Hindered by the self-centered blindness of youth, sadly I no longer gave my father the respect he deserved.

※ ※ ※

In time, maturity and my introduction to the gospel of Christ helped to clear my vision. It helped me see the realities of life for what they were. "Both abundance and lack exist simultaneously in our lives, as parallel realities. It is always our conscious choice which secret garden we will tend. . . . When we chose not to focus on what is missing from our lives but are grateful for the abundance that's present . . . the wasteland of illusion falls away and we experience Heaven on earth."[2]

Although my father would never again shine as brightly in my eyes as he had when I was a boy, I recognized the role his concerned hand had in my life. His stern direction to stay the course had not only kept me out of trouble as he hoped it would, but gave me strength and purpose to overcome the brutality of life that surrounded all of us in our community.

The opportunities provided made me stronger and more capable. Doors were opened I did not even know existed growing up in the Heights. But by then I had long since left my father's house and didn't take the time to express my gratitude to him. I suppose I thought he probably knew I appreciated him. I suppose I thought he knew I loved him. I suppose I thought myself too busy to tell him, too busy with more important things in life.

Looking back it is clear now we should never let our busy lives, our pride, or a disagreement to be resolved stand in the way of a parent, brother, or sister to be loved and gratitude expressed. Children grow up. Families move apart. Loved ones pass on. It is so easy to take them for granted until that day when they are no longer here with us, gone from our lives. We are left with feelings of "what if," "if only," or "why didn't I."

✳ ✳ ✳

Very early on a crisp fall Sunday morning, before the bustle of the day had begun, I sat alone with my father in the shadowy darkness of his hospice room. Shaken and apprehensive, I watched him struggle to take the final breaths of his mortal life. I knew it wouldn't be long before he joined those who had gone before. I recognized the discomforting rattle of death with each breath. And although I had known for some time this day was coming, I was not prepared to let him go.

I sat anxious by his bedside, he teetered precariously on the edge of mortality. The recognition of the sacrifice offered, the lessons taught, and the gratitude due became clear to my heart; the stark reality of the simple words of gratefulness still left unsaid. Tears began to course down my cheeks as I struggled along with my father in these, the final hours of his life on earth.

I tried to pull myself together. I couldn't. In my heart I felt conflicted, deeply troubled with the memory of my disrespectful youth and the guilt that lay heavy on my shoulders. I wrestled with the pending loss of my father and the need to cleanse my soul. Death can seem so cruel to loved ones left behind, especially when confronted unprepared. I stood and walked out of my father's hospice room.

I wandered aimlessly through the shadowy hallways in the early morning quiet, away from hospice rooms, away from death, and into the peaceful silence of a sleeping hospital. Deep in contemplation I pondered my pending loss, my regrets, my unacknowledged guilt.

Lost deep in thought, I recalled that long ago Christmas, the young confused and rebellious boy who idolized his father. Precious memories of my boyhood, my youth, and my many blessings in life filled my mind, when came the intruding cry of a newborn baby to break the quiet of the morning. This was a new life sent here by our Father in Heaven to begin his sojourn through his own time on earth.

With the cry of a newborn baby, the Lord had intervened to break the spell of my self-absorbed regret. This was a new life bringing joy and stirring all the hopes and dreams of young parents, reminiscent memories of grandparents and eliciting the best wishes of family and friends.

The cries of this newborn child had now brought to the forefront of my thoughts the sweet blessing of that first Christmas morning two millennia earlier. In that inspirational moment I felt my Father in Heaven lighten my burden, touch my heart and remind me both birth and death are all a part of His Plan. They are interwoven into the very fabric of His gospel, just as the birth of our Savior and His Atoning death and Resurrection are integrated inseparably one with the other. Christ's birth would not be celebrated without His death and Atonement.

The still small voice of the Spirit let me know the tears of death are part of the trial and beauty of the one life we have to live. "The only way to take sorrow out of death is to take love out of life."[3] I knew then what I must do.

I returned to my father's hospice room and prepared myself to give him his first and only blessing in this life. As my father struggled hard for each breath, I prayed for strength, wisdom, and the will of my Father in Heaven with the blessing He wanted me to deliver. I placed my hands on his head and stood silent for some time awaiting inspiration, feeling the rhythm of his life slipping away under my touch.

His breathing calmed. I gradually pulled myself together. I knew then this was the last moment in time I would share with my father on this earth. At long last, as the cool light of daybreak streamed silently through the window, the Spirit of the Lord entered my heart with the words I felt He wanted me to convey.

I expressed my love for my father, my appreciation for all he had given me in life leading to my many blessings. I thanked him for the lessons on the importance of strength of character, the blessings of hard work, the value of struggle to overcome life's challenge, the reward of self-reliance. I thanked him for the opportunities he gave me that led to receiving the gospel in my life. Most precious of all: the opportunities that led me to my beautiful wife, Anne, who even now as the ties that bind us to this earthly life become frayed and worn, I love more than ever. Finally, I thanked him for my children, whom I love so dearly.

I offered a blessing of hope and strength from the gospel of Christ to calm his fears—not a reassurance that all would be well, but instead a reminder of the gospel truths that he might cling to, carry with him beyond the veil, beyond the cares and toil of his earthly journey. I don't know if my father heard me. I often pray he did hear the gratitude spoken, for I certainly owed it to him.

It was a crushing few moments, there alone with my father in the early morning quiet as his gift of time on earth inconspicuously slipped away unnoticed by the world. My father, like most of us, had left no great name in life nor accomplished any great deeds to be remembered by, but his effect on my life was incalculable.

In the eyes of a young boy he had indeed been my hero, a great man who in part helped shape my perceptions of life growing up in America. Fatherhood to him was not a hobby. It was not something to do when he could squeeze in the time; it was a cornerstone in his life.

Frankly, parenting is one of the great gifts God gave us time on earth for, isn't it? Strength of character forged in life is partly dependent upon those unselfish, unhistoric acts by devoted parents, who quietly give their hidden lives to their children, then go to rest in unvisited graves.

In those final moments with my father, there was no confusion in my mind about what was most important in life, what I should be grateful for, or where to find my happiness. I didn't need to search for happiness in some far away land with a strange name. I had known for some time my happiness was right in front of me, in my own home, not in the precarious wasteland of illusion promulgated by the world.

For several minutes after the blessing was done and finished, I seemed unable to lift my hands to break this final bond between father and son. Then finally, I felt the reassuring, comforting spirit of the Lord encircle me with love: "Fear thou not, for I am with thee"[4] in your time of sorrow.

I sat alone by my father's side watching for some time as he slipped ever deeper into unconsciousness, but he was calm now and the end came quickly. There was an overwhelming desire deep within my soul to hold my own family tight; a powerful testimony of the reality of the Resurrection and the actuality that my father would still live beyond the grave and I would see him again.

* * *

In the quiet of the night, I sat alone with Anne in front of the fire that danced and crackled in the hearth. For some moments I sat without a word, reflecting on the day's events and pondering the passing of my father.

"Life is fleeting. It is for all of us, isn't it?" I said softly to Anne as we snuggled closer together in front of the flickering glow of the fire, listening to the cold, whispering wind outside. "There is no opportunity for a dress rehearsal. How does Thomas S. Monson put it? 'we laugh, we cry, we work, we play, we love, we live. And then we die. Death is our universal heritage. All must pass its portals. Death claims the aged, the weary and worn. It visits the youth in the bloom of hope and the glory of expectation. Nor are little children kept beyond its grasp.'[5]"

Anne turned to look at me with a touch of moisture in her eyes, "It's at times like this that the words of the Apostle Paul strike a sobering cord, 'It is appointed to all men once to die.'[6]" Then, snuggling into my shoulder and wrapping her arms around my arm as the embracing fire crackled before us, she added, "And that would be the end of it, wouldn't it, if it weren't for our Savior, born in Nazareth on that miraculous first Christmas, cradled in a rude manger amongst a stable of sheep. But this was only the beginning of the most profound gift God would ever give any of us. His birth fulfilled prophesies of the Old Testament of a Christ who would teach by example, reveal the full light of truth, the life to live and the path for all of us to follow," she so eloquently shared, "but it was Christ's Atonement that was the greatest gift."

"His was a power stronger than weapons; a wealth more lasting than the coins of Caesar. And the multitudes followed Him. Children adored Him. He lived an exemplary, perfect, and faultless life," I added to her stirring comments.

"But you're right after all this," Anne went on, "we must never forget that it was His Atonement that was His greatest gift. For if not for His Atonement, we would not be celebrating His birth on Christmas morning."

Anne snuggled closer, nestling her head further into my shoulder, and I added to her thought, "It must have broken His Father's heart to watch mankind greet His Only Begotten Son as an enemy, a conspirator, a traitor. Then to stand idly by while Jesus carried the entire burden on His shoulders as the charade of a trial unfolded, with their cries of 'Crucify Him! Crucify Him!' filling the air. Then to watch Him stagger alone on that long climb up Calvary Hill, while ridiculed, reviled, mocked, jeered, then finally nailed to a cross with shouts of 'He can save others, but he cannot save Himself.' I can't imagine it."

"And His mother," Anne said, "what must have passed through her mind and heart as she stood helpless, watching the events of that day unfold through tears of unimaginable despair? Who could possibly measure this mother's grief? With a perfect faith in God she had walked, her hand in His, into the valley of the shadow of death, to bring forth this beautiful baby boy on that first joyful Christmas morning. Hers was the Son of Man, a light unto all the world. Now exhausted and helpless, Mary watched her perfect son crucified for all mankind who at that moment seemed to have abandoned Him." Anne was quiet for a moment, then added, "Mary's sinless son was crucified for you and I, and your father, David." And with that Anne lifted her head to smile at me.

There was a pause in our conversation as together we watched the fire flicker, dance, and burn. It seemed the only light in that dark night.

"What must Mary and our Father in Heaven have felt at that poignant moment when their son pleaded for the forgiveness of His tormentors?" Anne added, her voice cracking. "Mary's heart must have ached beyond comprehension as she heard their only son's final words on this earth, 'Father, into thy hands I commend my spirit.'⁷ Mary's life with her flawlessly perfect son was no more!"

The thunder and darkness covered the whole earth as it trembled and shook in pain, then finally the angry clouds spilled a cleansing rain to wipe away that terrible night; leaving Mary with her son's lingering admonition, "Fear thou not; for I am with thee: be not dismayed; for I am thy God: I will strengthen thee; yea, I will help thee."⁸

I sat quiet for some moments staring at the dancing fire as it popped and crackled in the hearth, then added a final comment, "The world would never be the same, for Jesus broke the bonds of death. As we're told in Psalms, 'Weeping may endure for a night, but joy cometh in the morning.'⁹ And for the first time, the eyes of the Saints could see, their ears could hear, and their hearts could feel and understand the full mission of their Savior—to pay for the sins of all mankind, and herald the greatest miracle of time and eternity, that each of us may be resurrected with Him in the springtime of our lives."

✳ ✳ ✳

Life goes by so fast. May we always remember to slow down and enjoy it. Don't take each other for granted. Relish each and every moment—they're gone so quickly. The moments roll into minutes, hours, days, and years. Then one day we awaken to our last Christmas morning and the opportunity to share that spirit of Christmas is no more.

Tell your parents, your brothers, and your sisters how much you love and appreciate them. We never know how soon it will be too late. "The bitterest tears shed over graves are for words left unsaid and deeds left undone."[10] "Thank you." "I love you." "I'm so sorry." Each are such simple gifts, but with profound meaning to the receiver.

And above all remember, "God so loved the world, that he gave his only begotten Son, that whosoever believeth in him should not perish, but have everlasting life."[11]

That precious Son gave us His life, the Atonement that achieved victory over death for all of us—the cornerstone of all Christendom. God's Christmas gift became our Easter blessing. May every heart open wide and welcome Him; not only on Christmas Morning, but always.

"Merry Christmas to you all!"

*With tears of joy and gratitude running down her face, Stephanie sat in the
middle of her new rug, in her freshly painted living room, taking in
all that her children, friends, and neighbors had done out of love for her.*

# The Thin Line between Giver and Receiver

One of the greatest lessons life can teach is the art of distinguishing between what is important and what is not. Unfortunately, sometimes our busy lives are embroiled in the thick of thin things, and we miss the opportunity to align our actions with our good intentions. Recall with me the old adage, "I can't hear what you're saying, because your actions speak louder than your words." The question we must ask ourselves: "Do we act on our best charitable intentions when the opportunity comes our way, or do we wait until another day?" The Christmas season often seems to help clarify our vision, to motivate us to make a difference in the lives of those around us, not just talk about it.

It is during the Christmas season when we are especially cognizant of the importance of charity, when we are more keenly aware of the Savior's admonition to love our neighbor with compassion and longsuffering. It is the one time of year when we seem to recognize the world is but a looking glass, reflecting back on us the kindness and charity we show our fellow man. Often it's simple acts of service, things so slight and seemingly insignificant that they are impossible to count in dollars and cents. Simple gifts that may cost little, or often no money at all, yet the comfort, joy, and blessings these kindnesses give can sometimes make all the difference, as if they cost a fortune. This active love for one another is an essential element of Christ's message, bringing us closer to God, and the miracle of Christmas!

✳ ✳ ✳

Several years ago, when my daughter Rachel was going to high school, she had a boyfriend named Ryan. While joining us for dinner at our home one evening, Ryan shared a concern for his family. His father, rather than face the responsibility of providing for a family in turmoil, had left Ryan's mother to fend for herself, her three adolescent children, and one adult child away at college. Because of this family tragedy, their life had gotten very complicated, filled with financial distress, heartache, and despair. They had been left destitute.

Stephanie, who had spent the past twenty years as a stay-at-home mom raising four children, no longer had any money or means of financial support. She was late on her mortgage, in debt to more creditors than she could count, and her utilities had recently been cut off. It was a very difficult and trying time for her family. Stephanie's heart was so full of sorrow and heartache she felt sure it would break.

Ryan, a college-bound athlete in his last semester of high school, tried admirably to fill the role of the man in the house for the sake of his mom and two younger sisters. He was a special young man, and though he did his best to fill the void, Ryan was not yet ready for this heavy responsibility.

Nevertheless, Ryan took a part-time job instead of competing in sports. Determined to provide for her family, Stephanie did her best to pull herself together, dust off her twenty-year-old resume, and was lucky enough to find a part-time job at her children's Catholic School teaching physical education. Then shortly after found, she had an advanced case of cancer.

It was only by the grace of God that she obtained limited health insurance through her work before hearing of the diagnosis. Still she had little money to pay the costly deductibles on the expensive medical bills and care for a busy household.

The family pulled together and lent a hand wherever they could to ease the burden on Stephanie. When it came time to head for college, Ryan turned down offers for college athletic scholarships and stayed home to help with the household needs and other family financial obligations. It broke Stephanie's heart to see her loving son set his life on hold for her and her girls, but what could she do?

By late fall, it was clear Stephanie would have to undergo a double mastectomy followed by weeks of chemotherapy. All in the family focused on Stephanie and the challenges she was facing in her fight against cancer. Everything else was secondary. The house had fallen into severe disrepair from years of children growing up within its walls and neglect. There was virtually no food in the cupboards. The yard was full of weeds and left unwatered to save the cost.

One early December evening while driving home from work, I couldn't help but think about Stephanie and her family. We had grown close to Ryan and his mom. Anne frequently brought in dinners and spent long hours with Stephanie during her chemotherapy, helping her cope with the challenges of raising a family and of never having enough money to take care of what needed to be done around the house—plumbing problems, electrical issues, roof leaks, peeling paint, and heaven forbid if the subject of landscaping came up.

We could all see Stephanie's life crumbling down around her. I tried to push it from my mind as I drove down the highway. "This is not my business," I told myself. "I'm very busy with work, my own family and soon with three in college. It is a struggle with my own challenges in life." But the Lord has a way of touching the heart of even the least of His children, for imperfect people are all He has to work with. It must be awfully frustrating, but after days of prompting, I finally decided to see if there was something we might do to ease the burden on this good neighbor, Stephanie and her family. The Christmas season was in full swing and something needed to be done so this wonderful family might have a meaningful Christmas. They certainly deserved it!

✳ ✳ ✳

I first called Ryan to discuss with him the possibilities of a "house make-over," a Christmas present to Stephanie and her family. "It might make life a bit more comfortable for your mom after her long weeks of chemotherapy," I told Ryan. He was deeply touched and fully behind the idea, except for two concerns: cost and how to keep his mom out of the house during the remodel. I promised the cost wouldn't be a problem and agreed the disruption to Stephanie's life during construction would hardly be a Christmas present.

Ryan suggested a recuperation trip for his mom to Texas spending time with her sister after her long struggle going through chemotherapy. Her sister had already offered to help in any way she could. "It could be a two-week vacation before Christmas," Ryan plotted. "Of course we wouldn't tell her about the planned home makeover!"

Ryan brought Stephanie's sister in on the clandestine plan, who thought it a wonderful idea and took to it from the start. "We can go to the spa, a concert or two, Christmas shopping, or just relax if that is all she is up for. We'll give her a break from life and responsibility for a time, a respite to help speed up her recovery, all expenses paid."

Rachel and Anne were excited about the plan. Stephanie would fly to her sister's home in Texas for a little well-deserved rest and recuperation, then return for Christmas. During her absence the family and neighbors would tackle her home to surprise her when she returned. Hopefully it would be a pleasant surprise. "After all, isn't this the best way to have a good Christmas," I reminded our family, "to forget yourself and help put a little Christmas cheer in someone else's life?"

I called the bishop of our congregation. We enlisted the other church leaders and went about putting the details of the plan together to help this wonderful family in their time of need. Ryan was overwhelmed by the willingness of our congregation to reach out to someone who was not of their faith and whom most did not even know.

"It is an opportunity to be charitable to our friends who need it, regardless of your faith," the bishop shared with Ryan. "All of us from time to time are in need of a helping hand and yours is a wonderful family who deserves one."

As is often the result of following Christ's commandments, blessings came to our family and those in the community who had the opportunity to plan, organize, and implement the work party over the Christmas holidays in equal measure. This heart-warming experience drew us all closer together as family, friends, community, and of course, Stephanie's children.

After years of neglect while raising four children on a shoestring, Stephanie's home needed some tender loving care. Carpet, paint, lumber, roof tile, and drywall were all contributed free or at drastically discounted prices and friends donated what money was needed to make ends meet.

It was an inspiring time for all of us, to see brothers and sisters, parents, friends, and neighbors, Ryan and his sisters working shoulder to shoulder. We tore out the old and replaced it with the new, framing walls, hanging drywall, taping, plastering, roofing, cleaning, and painting, then laying beautiful new carpet in every room.

The women of our congregation reorganized the kitchen. Their teenagers, Ryan's sisters and friends, neighbors, and members from Stephanie's church cleaned the cabinets and then filled them with food of every kind, as well as pots and pans, cooking utensils, dishes, and silverware.

Boys stripped and leveled both the front and back yards, then replanted them under Anne's guiding hand. And the girls from the rather affluent local high school donated clothes for the two girls for which they were forever grateful.

Our family all dug in, especially Rachel who became a task master, ordering Ryan's football buddies here and there, taking charge of many of the tasks and making it her personal goal to see the project was done right and we endured to the end to make Stephanie's house into a beautiful home again.

Seeing these newfound friends building bonds for a lifetime with one another was an inspiring sight; it was a labor of love. There are no words to describe the heartfelt gratitude we all had for this opportunity to provide a little Christmas cheer into the life of this wonderful lady and her family. After all, the best way to put a little joy into your own life is to bring a little to someone else's.

When our work was finished, we all stood back in appreciation of what had been accomplished. Holes had been filled and were freshly painted, broken tiles were all replaced to keep out the rain, new entry railings had been built, and there was a beautifully mowed lawn with flowers in new planters stretching forth in the afternoon sun. Ryan, his sisters, and the rest of us smiled at the beautiful rebirth of their wonderful little home. We each savored the priceless feeling that comes with real service for a good cause and hoped Stephanie would be pleased with our Christmas present she so rightly deserved.

"Merry Christmas, Stephanie," Rachel so aptly expressed as we looked for a last time at our shared offering to Stephanie, who would arrive home in a couple days. "Merry Christmas from all of us, and thank you for making our Christmas the best ever!"

✳ ✳ ✳

Stephanie arrived that evening tired, but looking forward to seeing her children. This was the longest time she had ever been separated from them. She was excited when Ryan and the girls picked her up at the airport. The reunion was heartfelt and emotional. Sure she had enjoyed her time away being pampered and spoiled, but she was delighted to be back with her beautiful children. And they reciprocated that feeling to their mom. "We're so excited to see you, Mom," came from the girls. Ryan, in his quiet and steady way, leaned down to give her a welcoming hug and a kiss. "I love you, Mom. We missed you." This brought uncontrolled tears to her eyes. Families can be such a wonderful healing balm.

Of course, Ryan and the girls couldn't wait to get home before the sun went down. Stephanie was a bit surprised when they turned down dinner, especially when she promised ice cream after. "This is a little unusual," she told them, smiling. "Things must have changed more than I expected while I've been gone!" That caused her youngest to giggle and Ryan to give his little sister a disapproving glance.

There are just not words enough to describe the look on Stephanie's face when Ryan pulled up in front of the house. Astonishment, amazement, bewilderment, astonished wonder. None of these words quite captured it. She was left speechless. Frankly, at first she could not believe her eyes.

She would later describe her first impression after acknowledging that this was indeed not a dream: "It was the most wonderful Christmas present ever. That was until I opened the front door and saw the inside of my newly refurbished little home. Tears began to stream down my cheeks as I hugged my children one by one, who were all crying too. We were all a mess," she said, smiling. "I went from one room to another shocked anew each time, asking my children how did this all happened," Stephanie said. "After making an absolute fool of myself sobbing uncontrollably, I finally calmed down enough to remember it was well after dinner time and I should make something for my family. I opened the normally empty fridge and then the cupboards, and I started to cry all over again. I didn't know what to do I was so happy, so I just sat in the middle of my new beautifully carpeted family room floor and cried, thanking God for friends and family."

I told my children, "If I die this very moment, I will be a happy woman. I love you so!"

✳ ✳ ✳

When we first heard the details from Ryan, it warmed our hearts with inexpressible love and compassion, more than any other Christmas present we could have received. And what did it cost us, a few dollars and a little time well spent? It was worth every penny, every minute and much more. Stephanie later gave each member of our family a tearful hug and a kiss. The memory of that electric moment, the shared love, the warmth for one another, and the happiness and joy we each felt will forever remain lodged in a special corner of our hearts as this wonderful family allowed us to be a part of their lives.

For Christmas, our family was privileged to watch Ryan give his mom a check to pay the deductible for her chemotherapy. He had earned it working many long nights, courtesy of the San Diego Chargers. It was a magnificent expression of love on all sides.

The beautiful Christ child was born on Christmas day two centuries earlier, and His message still warms our hearts these many centuries later. His birth, life, and sacrifice would make it possible for this family to be together forever. How fortunate we all are.

※ ※ ※

Unfortunately Stephanie's condition continued to deteriorate. For months, while Stephanie struggled with her cancer, the women of our church, neighbors, and friends from hers coordinated efforts to bring food most every night, help with chores, pay utility bills, and bring cheerful tidings. Anne spent countless hours helping and counseling Stephanie through her difficult, tearful, emotional times. Stephanie and Anne were only neighbors, but they loved each other like sisters just the same. They would remain eternal friends to the end.

I will never forget the night Stephanie, though not of our faith, asked the bishop and me for a blessing. The cancer had progressed and she was concerned for her family and as were all of us. She was hoping for a miracle.

The Spirit was so strong as the blessing rolled out to this beautiful lady—touching, reassuring, and calming. Not that all would be well, but preparing her for passing from this life. It was an offering of hope and strength to her loving family, calming their fears, preparing them for the eventuality of her moving beyond the cares and toil of her earthly journey. "The miracle," the bishop sweetly shared, "is the birth, the life, and the

Atonement of Jesus Christ and his gift of Eternal Life, a gift you shall surely receive."

Tears were shed, hugs exchanged between mother and daughter, mother and son, and eternal friends. There was no confusion about what was most important in life as we held fast to each other. The line between the giver and the receiver was blurred that day.

Stephanie passed away in the spring and was buried among the beautiful flowers as Easter approached.

※ ※ ※

What Matters Most? To the grieving Martha, Christ comforted: "I am the resurrection, and the life: he that believeth in me, though he were dead, yet shall he live: And whosoever liveth and believe in me shall never die."[1] Times change, the years roll by, circumstances vary, but the Masters counsel to Martha applies to me and to you just as surely as though we heard his voice speaking directly to us. He who taught us to love God with all our hearts, and with all our strength, and with all our mind, and our neighbors as ourselves, is a teacher of truth.

May each of us remember our Savior was born on Christmas morning and invite him and His message into our homes as part of our Christmas celebration. And may we partake of the wonder and fulfillment of Christian service by setting aside convenience and obligation, personal comfort and pleasure, for the heart-warming blessings of charity. For as the ancient prophet so succinctly acknowledged, when we are in the service of our neighbors, we are surely in the service of our God.

*Brothers forever; the best things in*
*life are not really things at all!*

# Families Are Forever

*M*any years ago, our oldest, a shy but very determined ten-year-old, became fascinated with everything baseball. Michael often spent hours, in the quiet of his room, studying his thousands of baseball cards and reading magazine stories of his boyhood heroes. Sometimes on summer afternoons with his buddies and often Dad, he played out his imaginations in sandlot ball games on the schoolyard down the street from our home. His particular specialty, as it was for many young boys: imagined grand slam home runs. He'd circle the bases in his most affected home run trot to the imaginary applause of adoring fans, politely doffing his hat in mock appreciation.

We sometimes played into the evening twilight and on the walk home shared stories of the great players of the game, both past and present. It was the best of times. It was a time of innocence for my boys.

One spring, Alley's Restaurant chain in San Diego had a contest offering some lucky young boy the opportunity of a lifetime—to catch fly balls in center field at Padre's Stadium on the final day of the season. Michael was determined to win this contest. All through the summer he made his daily stop at Alley's, stuffing the ballot box with applications. Each time he would leave his ballot with the young hostess accompanied by his cutest boyish smile in the hope to sway the jury, a smile that was destined for trouble in later years.

To everyone's surprise and especially to Dad, Michael won the drawing. He was so excited. Determined to hone his fly ball catching skills to the absolute pinnacle of perfection before the big day, he coaxed a friend into setting up the pitching machine in the grocery store parking lot to shoot baseballs high in the air. As they drifted down, he locked the baseball into his tractor beam, hauling in each catch with two-handed precision. He practiced hour after hour, day after day, until he had it perfect.

The day came. And on a warm fall afternoon, Michael and I were escorted through the catacombs of Qualcomm Stadium. As we stepped onto the field, Michael saw for the very first time the five shiny new cars to be given away that day, and the 55,000 fans there just for that purpose.

My heart sank as I looked into the wide eyes of my shy little boy, filled with awe and frankly a bit of terror, as he saw all those fans in the stands looking down on him.

I took up residence in the Padres dugout, standing in casual conversation with Tim Flannery as Michael made the long walk into deep center field alone. Almost the entire Padre team sat leisurely stretching on the summer grass in centerfield. They casually looked on, watching as the preparation for the Alley's Restaurant event unfolded. As with many young boys, these were Michael's idols. He knew every name of every player, their batting averages, ERA, home run stats—all of it. There was no statistic that escaped his meticulous scrutiny in the quiet of his room as he combed through his baseball cards over and over again.

Jerry Coleman, the Padres announcer, introduced Michael to a very raucous crowd. If he caught all three balls, each of the fans would receive a free meal at Alley's Restaurant, and if he caught only one, a free dessert. Just what this shy young boy needed, a little more added pressure? He stood all alone in center field, anxiously looked at me standing by the dugout along the third base line, then up at the fans behind me. Row after row of 55,000 fans staring back at him. I could see panic in his eyes and my heart ached for him.

He readied himself. The first ball was shot high into the air, almost out of sight before it started its floating descent back down to earth. But these were not baseballs. These were cloth balls drifting back and forth in the fall breeze that circled in centerfield. Michael looked skyward following the ball this way and that, deep in concentration before the ball hit the heel of his glove and fell to the ground. He stood petrified, staring at the ball lying there on the ground. Frightened disbelief flashed across his face as the crowd in unison, gave out a great "OOOHHH" of disappointment. Once more he tried to make the catch without success. On Michael's final attempt , his boyhood hero Tony Gwynn lent his helping hands and an encouraging word, which made this final failure to catch the ball all the more heartbreaking. Michael was devastated. The crowd's instinctive reaction to his three-time failure to catch the fly balls echoed their displeasure.

I saw in my son's pale blue eyes the wrenching, desperate disappointment. Tears trickled down his cheeks as he struggled to bring his emotions under control to at least retain his dignity. He made the long walk from center field to the foul line and to my side. He wiped his eyes. I put my arm around his shoulder and we made the infinitely longer walk back down the foul line toward the dugout, then through the catacombs under the field. Unflattering comments from young boys and irreverent fans followed us along the long painful walk out of the stadium and into the parking lot for a quiet moment together.

Thoughts raced through my mind as we walked. I felt woefully ill equipped for the teaching moment that lay ahead. "Don't mess this up, Dad," I told myself. I could think of so many other fathers better prepared. But this moment was mine to own—to be a father as best I could. I couldn't delegate or pass it off to someone better qualified. I said a little prayer in my heart as we walked to the parking lot, our car, a quiet place to talk. "Father in Heaven, I wish I was a better man. Please, I'm gonna need your help here."

For the better part of an hour we talked. Michael expressed his searing disappointment, his embarrassment, his pain, and all the emotions that come with failure.

I let him know how proud I was of him for his unrelenting determination, for facing his fears, for taking the leap, and risking it all.

I shared with him moments in my own boyhood when I to had failed—the agony of defeat and self-loathing I went through trying to make sense of it.

"But I have learned failure is just a part of life," I told him. "Even when we put forth our best effort, we sometimes fail. Sometimes things turn out just downright awful. Sometimes it is hard to understand why this happens. Sometimes it is difficult to see the light at the end of the tunnel."

These many years later I have learned failure is oftentimes the best teacher. Through failure we learn to better face our fears, to overcome our emotions, to master the challenges of life. Failure is often the best teacher to prepare us with the confidence to succeed next time. Failure is frequently the greatest character builder we are given in life. "The pain will pass. This experience will make you stronger," I told him. "Success is often one failure after another, long enough until finally we get it right."

＊＊＊

Life is not a dress rehearsal. The opportunities for fathers to teach their young sons and daughters come, and then they're gone. When it's time to perform this sacred task, the time for preparation is over. We as fathers must be there in heart, mind, and spirit, prepared for those teaching moments. Don't miss them. You'll regret it. As the poet John Greenleaf Whittier wrote, "For of all sad words of tongue or pen, The saddest are these: "It might have been!""[1]

Every part of raising children is humbling. We all make our share of mistakes. And frankly some mistakes are just too good to make only once. Our children are frequently kind enough to remind us of those mistakes and of particular importance to children, are our shortcomings just in case we might forget. Mine have all been enshrined in the "Remember What Dad Did When" hall of shame. I know where the land mines are now, because I have stepped on all of them. I was often too tense, obsessive, and over the top.

I wish I had not been in such a hurry to get on to the next thing. I wish I had treasured the doing a little more and getting it done a little less; savored the precious teaching moments, listened to the spirit, reveled in the uniqueness of each beautiful child that God has given us. I wish I had taken them fishing more often.

The truth is, like most fathers, I worried over our children constantly, wondering if I was spending enough one on one time, being supportive enough, or too much, teaching the right lessons, saying the right thing to make their hurts better or just plain missing out on those fleeting opportunities? What lessons were they learning from my example? Were they even listening to what I thought at the time was sage advice?

The truth is I never seemed to have enough time to satisfy my work demands, to figure out how to pay the bills, fulfill my church assignments, coach that soccer game, help with homework, the merit badge, attend that ballet performance, or the torturous piano recital. I just tried to disappoint as infrequently as possible.

Sometimes we fathers have to smile, just to keep from losing it. Being a father is exhausting, humbling, and often humiliating, and it is worth every single minute of it. I wouldn't trade those moments to surf a million perfect waves all to myself. And no matter how old my children are, I will always be their father, always married to their mother.

Now in our golden years, which sometimes seemed to be laced with lead, it is touching and rewarding to see the love of our children reflected in the sacrifice they each make for those in their own families. Especially at Christmas time. There is no better time than Christmas time to see their kind, considerate, and charitable giving. There is nothing that brings more joy to the spirit of Christmas than to watch the sacrifice, forgiveness, and gratitude shared between each other in their own families.

✳ ✳ ✳

In our current cultural climate, it is now crystal clear why our Father in Heaven provided us with the guiding principles in the "The Family: The Proclamation to the World." We hold in our arms the rising generation. They come to this Earth facing unparalleled challenges, with limitless untapped capabilities, and great spiritual opportunities.

You cannot be casual about how you prepare these beautiful children our Father in Heaven has lent us. It's for just a short time really.

We fathers must do all you can to be prepared for those teaching moments: study the words of Christ, humble ourselves, get down on our knees to pray for our Father in Heaven's help, not just in our desperate time of need, but often. Have the faith He will be there with us; to help us with our children's successes, their failures; to help teach them the principals of overcoming loss; to build their character, self reliance, and an understanding that free agency must be coupled with personal responsibility.

Help them to understand they may be old enough to make choices, but not to determine the consequences. And when they fall, be there to help them get back up and try again.

It is our obligation to be the best father we can be; arm our children for battle against the unrivaled challenges this rising generation will surely face; help them stand tall for their God-given inalienable right and freedom to "choose the right," to fight for their liberty in a world where parents and children are often confused as we slide toward social anarchy. We must teach our sons and daughters how to hold their families close; to build a relationship with their Savior, precept upon precept.

✳✳✳

Now may I take a moment to speak of the most important role in the family—mothers. To quote Dr. Stuart Rosenberg, a noted child psychologist, "the role of a mother is the most crucial to the successful development of a child into a responsible and caring adult." There is a crisis of leadership in our country today when it comes to families and the role of women. It is a modern misconception that motherhood and raising a family is somehow less important and less fulfilling than pursuing a career. An intolerant, unholy, cultural alliance has discounted motherhood as an archaic and unfulfilling vocation to the detriment of women, families, and all of society frankly.

Women are innately equipped to care for their children in ways that we as fathers don't fully understand really. Mothers must not be distracted by a culture advocating moral confusion. I need only ask my daughter Rachel, a high school English teacher, of the impact on struggling teens who don't have a strong, empathetic, and nurturing mother in the home,

*The quiet, invisible hand of a loving mother will be
felt through generations still to come.*

to understand why there are so many self-centered, irresponsible, inse-
cure, dysfunctional adults in our midst.

At times, the invisibility of a mother's work within the walls of her
own home might feel like a burden. But remember this: the health of a
nation, the happiness of its people, their prosperity, and their peace all
find common roots in a mother teaching her children in the home. If you,
as mothers can keep the right perspective in mind, you can see yourselves
as great builders, whose imprint on your child will be left on generations
to come.

※ ※ ※

"Children are an heritage of the Lord."[2] "The Family: The Proclamation to
the World" further clarifies: "Husband and wife have a solemn responsibility to first love and care for each other, then for their children. Mothers,
with the most important and sacred role are primarily responsible for the
nurture and teaching of their children; fathers have the primary responsibility to provide for the temporal needs of the family; fathers and mothers
are obligated to help one another as equal partners."[3]

Education in the lives of our children should not stop at the school-
house door. Mothers and fathers in the in the gospel of Christ understand
the importance of teaching children about standards, values, gospel doctrine, self-reliance, personal responsibility and about life frankly. We must
understand, instilling values is our imperative duty that we owe the rising
generation.

The emotional and spiritual events shared as a family: learning,
laughing, struggling and even crying create a rich and enduring bond of
intimacy that helps carry us through life's challenges and build unbreak-
able friendships within the bonds of family. The biggest mistake we make
as parents is not considering "What would the Lord want me to do with
this teaching moment?"

Among the many things I have learned as a father raising children is
to try to understand the best things in life are not really things at all, nor
are they seen or heard, but felt through the Spirit, the still small voice that
sheds the light of Christ on our lives. The gospel of Christ is where the
answers are to be found, to raising a family, or solving the world's problems. This understanding is particularly clear now that our children are
grown, and the moments are gone, captured only in my memories.

Despite the many challenges facing families in this the twenty-first century, the payoff of a strong, loving family is worth any price. I cherish the uniqueness of all four of my now-grown children, their near-perfect spouses, and my absolutely perfect grandchildren. These are my very best friends. And, of course, above all there is my lovely wife, Anne. I testify to you of the truthfulness of the scripture: "For what shall it profit a man, if he shall gain the whole world, and lose his own soul" and family?[4] Harold B. Lee and David O McKay probably said it best: "The greatest work we will ever do will be within the walls of our own home"[5] and "No success in life can compensate for failure in the family."[6]

The quiet, invisible hand of a loving mother, the example of a caring father to his children, and the strength of a gospel-centered home provide a safe harbor from the storms of the world and a place of refuge from the destructive whims of a confused society. Our families are an integral part of Christ's work, to bring to pass the happiness of man. "Train up a child in the way he should go: and when he is old, he will not depart from it."[7]

❋ ❋ ❋

There is an epilogue to the story of fly balls in the outfield. After Michael and I finished our father-son talk in the car, we walked back into the stadium to find his buddies and little brother enjoying the game like only boys can—no matter what their age. They were not the least bit concerned about Michael's debacle, or at least they made Michael feel that way. As is absolutely paramount while watching a baseball game we loaded up on the essentials: Padre dogs, ice cream, peanuts, Cracker Jacks, and popcorn. All the things boys need to keep their spirits up while watching their team lose yet another close one, at least until they slog back to the car holding their stomachs. When all was well, I slipped away to the Padre's stadium promotion office for a short conversation with the promotions director.

Near the end of the game an usherette showed up at our seats with a sweet smile, to see how the boys were enjoying the game and to invite Michael, his brother Paul, and the rest of us to join Tony Gwynn and the team in the player's parking lot after the game. Of course Michael was thrilled when we arrived and Tony Gwynn presented him with a game ball signed by the entire Padres team. Michael was so excited—it was almost worth missing the fly balls in the outfield.

Years later, little brother Paul and Dad sat down to lunch with Tony Gwynn to talk about Paul's prospects to play for the Padres after college baseball. As one father to another, I reminded Tony of the day he made missing three balls in the outfield all worthwhile for my boys.

May we always remember, "Families are forever"!

*By the end of every game, Paul was covered in dirt from head to toe except for his shiny white thumb—from sucking it in between innings, of course.*

# The Road Less Traveled

From the very first moment Paul set foot on the T-Ball field, it was clear to him what his vocation in life would be. It was carved in stone as far as he was concerned. He was going to be a professional baseball player and no amount of discouragement from the older, wiser boys, or explanations as to why it just couldn't be so from the all-knowing adults, was going to make any difference at all.

Do you know what the T in T-Ball stands for? It's torture. Torture for the parents who have to sit through two hours of watching four-year-old boys run around the base path on a baseball field, often in the wrong direction. But watching Paul play T-Ball was an entirely new jaw-dropping experience. He was fearless. He played the game with reckless abandon with no apparent concern for his own safety, or anyone else's for that matter. He risked life and limb at every opportunity. Frankly, it was usually the life and limb of the other guy at the greatest risk. Sometimes it was opponents, sometimes teammates, and sometimes even Coach, usually his dad, who paid the price for his overenthusiastic, aggressive play, and reckless abandon on the ball field. It wasn't that Paul was malicious—it was just Paul being Paul.

Paul played third base, shortstop, second, and first, which in and of itself wasn't particularly unusual, except with Paul, he played them all at once. He wanted to get every ball, make every out, launch himself head first into every base, and was hell-bent on stretching every hit into a home run as little boys, ball in hand, chased him around the bases. By the end of each game there wasn't a square inch of his little body that wasn't covered in dirt, except of course his thumb, which remained shiny-white like new snow on a bright sunny day from sucking it in between plays.

As for the T for torture, well, it took on a whole new meaning for the wide-eyed moms gasping at the sight of their sweet little boys sprawled out across the base path or laid out around the in-field after Paul had mowed them down like a freight train smashing copper pennies. But try as they might, it was difficult for those moms to get too upset with Paul. There he stood, feet spread wide apart, his shiny-white thumb tucked under his two remaining front teeth left blackened from an earlier fall. The cutest little boy you ever saw, with a mischievous twinkle in his eye and infectious smile spread wide across his face. Paul was entirely without guile—a delightful little boy, giddy with joy for the love of the game. To say baseball was Paul's passion would require a whole new definition of the word.

Paul rose through the ranks of youth baseball with distinction, finishing high school as "All Everything" in San Diego county, setting records along the way and receiving a scholarship to play college baseball at one of the most prestigious universities in the country with an athletic program to match.

Paul left for college a brash young ball player with two goals on his mind: play first string on the baseball team, and date every cute girl on campus. But his bishop had other plans for him. He secretly prayed that Paul might not have such a successful freshman year, humble himself, and be ready for a church mission that following summer.

Paul played well enough that year, and when it came time for a mission he received a lot of advice on why he shouldn't go. "It just isn't the right thing to do for his baseball career," advised Coach Machado to his father. "Talk him out of this foolishness and get him to call off his journey." But it wasn't to be; Paul had been touched by the Spirit. He prayed, and the scripture flooded into his mind "be still, and know that I am God,"[1] and all will be well. That was fair enough for him and with a promise to his coaches to get up extra early each morning and train before the day started, Paul after six weeks of language training headed for the Amazon jungles of Brazil just before Thanksgiving.

He quickly found there were not many living along the Amazon River who could catch a 90 mph fastball, and getting up at 4:30 a.m. each morning to train made it difficult to stay awake during the day. He even fell asleep in the middle of teaching. So it was back on his knees. "Father in Heaven, you wouldn't believe it. There are so many families here who are miserable and need the gospel in their lives. I want to do something for them. I want to bring the joy and blessing of the gospel of Jesus Christ to their lives."

Again, Paul was certain of his Father in Heaven's advice: "Lose yourself in the work and all will be well. Forget the training until you return from your mission." And so it was. Paul did just that, launched himself into the work just as he had with baseball and marveled at the Lord's hand in the lives of all those he touched.

\* \* \*

One evening, only two days before Christmas, Paul and his companion, Thomas, were walking home after a long day of trying to share their gospel message of Jesus Christ and the coming celebration of his birth. Even at night the heat and humidity was stifling along the Amazon equator. They were tired and their feet hurt from the many miles of walking the wet streets in battered shoes with holes worn right through the soles. It had been one of those discouraging days when the entire city of Belem, Brazil, seemed uninterested in their Christmas message of the Savior, favoring instead a party mood filled with drinking and more self-indulgent entertainment.

They turned away from the city, taking a back road shortcut home, when they came upon a family encamped in the rudest of shelters, jutting out from the banks of a small tributary to the great Amazon River, the jungle intruding in from all sides. Only in the most base of terms could it be called a home, cardboard walls, bits of wood, sheets of plastic, and a palm thatched roof, all tied together with lengths of rope.

It was not someplace they wanted to stop that evening, yet there was something about it. They both felt inspired to go to the door and knock on this very poor family's home.

A small olive-skinned girl with tangled black hair and beautiful large dark brown eyes answered, followed close behind by a young woman, presumably her mother. In his best Portuguese, Paul introduced himself and Thomas, "We have come with a Christmas message of our Savior, Jesus Christ. Would you like to hear it?"

With tired, but kind and welcoming, eyes the young woman answered with a warm smile, "Please, you look tired. Come in and rest your feet for a while," she offered in a lilting mix of Portuguese and a native Amazon dialect.

They both thanked her for her gracious invitation as they entered her home, then sat on the swept dirt floor. The walls were thin panels of scavenged corrugated plastic and heavy cardboard, placed wide apart, leaving openings to the outside between each panel. Sheets and makeshift pillows temporarily filled in these openings until they were needed for bedding when the cooler night air was allowed in.

The cooking facilities consisted of a small round fire ring of rock dug into one corner of the room, absent an exhaust to vent smoke from the fire to the outside. There was a peculiar collection of mismatched dishes—cracked, damaged, and chipped. Well used and dented pots stacked beside an old Styrofoam ice chest completed the kitchen.

The ramshackle shanty included an outside shower and wash bin fed by a cistern collecting rainwater and mounted haphazardly on the thrown together thatched roof. Together with a pit in the ground for the toilet, this served as their bathroom.

There was no furniture in the one room hovel, for it was filled to the brim with five of the cutest little smiling, dark-eyed children Paul had ever seen. Their proud mother, Maria, introduced each of the small children to the two missionaries and all courteously smiled back in recognition of their guests.

Paul, new to the work, was deeply touched by the extreme poverty of this struggling family. No one had shoes. Their homespun clothes were poorly fitted, threadbare hand-me-downs, obviously mended many, many times over the years.

The two missionaries smiled and greeted each child, showing them their best magic tricks and playing games to the children's delight. All were endearing, mischievous, and charming little mites, who laughed, giggled and ran around the room as they played with the two young Americans until finally Maria put the children down to bed.

Maria told them how the children's father had found work that day and was still at it. "No, he hadn't had much schooling or learned a trade. He will do any kind of work to support his family often late into the night," she said, "but he just can't seem to find much of it and all of his wages are spent on food and clothing for our family. We have not even been able to afford a marriage license. It's only love that keeps our family together."

"Of course there is no money for Christmas," she told them, "but I have used the Acai from the jungle and honey from hives along the river to make two bowls of sweet Acai for the children's Christmas. It's not much, but it will have to do." She proudly pointed to the delicacy curing on the open windowsill.

Paul and Thomas learned a lot about this family on that first night. Thanking Maria for the gracious hospitality, they left mother and family and continued on their walk home.

Later that night, as Paul lay in his bed, he thought about this family and the bleak Christmas in front of them. "Surely there must be something we can do to brighten Christmas for these children?" Paul asked Thomas.

The next morning, both raided their Christmas care packages received from their families back home, collecting granola bars, candy, gum, and a pocket knife. Then each went through all their drawers, pockets, and shelves collecting what little money they could find, coins mostly, for they too had little, living a very Spartan life in a humble but clean, one-room, concrete block room with cracked and broken concrete floors.

As soon as the local shops opened, they hurried into town to purchase all the candies, trinkets, and simple toys their money could buy, then wrapped each with packing paper.

That evening, Paul and Thomas went again to see the family with their gifts packed snugly away in their backpacks. They knocked. This time, Maria opened the door wide and invited them in. They stepped inside greeting each of the children by name. Each smiled and giggled asking to play games again. The missionaries smiled back, but this time they let the children know, "We are here on special assignment from Santa, who has been detained in the North Pole. He's very busy on Christmas Eve, you know."

All the children sat on the floor staring up at the two missionaries, fascinated by their message. Paul opened his backpack. "Santa has asked if we might stop by your home and drop off a couple things for him," he began, at which point he pulled out a small wrapped toy from his backpack and looked down at one of the wide-eyed little children.

"You must have been a very good boy, Alejandro, because look what Santa has sent this Christmas," Paul said as he handed a small present to the little boy, who shouted with glee as he tore through the wrapping paper.

"And you, young lady, must have been a very special princess, because look at this little doll he sent you, Francesca!" Her beautiful eyes, wide and sparkling, yielded to a contagious smile that spread wide across her brightening face.

One by one, Paul and Thomas pulled out their presents, handing them to each of the excited recipients. Each got his or her own special Christmas gift. With squeals of glee that would cause even Scrooge to smile, the children laughed and hugged their one-night Santa replacements.

In a solemn quiet, Mom looked on, her eyes filled with silent tears of thanksgiving. At first, arms folded to her chest with a hand over her mouth so that her emotions might not escape, she could not utter a word. Then she took Paul's hand with both of hers, looked into his eyes, and her face lit up with an infectious smile that melted his heart. She tried to choke back the tears, but she couldn't. The tears coursed down her cheeks until finally she offered a simple "Thank you!" It was the best she could do.

Then she grabbed both of Thomas's hands, took a deep breath, and burst out a profuse expression of her gratitude. "You are both so kind! You have made my children so happy."

The children's father, Joseph, reach out and shook the head of the two Americans. "My family will never forget you or this Christmas."

In a moment of inspiration, Maria offered, "May I also give you both a gift?" She reached toward the open windowsill, picked up the two bowls of honey-sweetened Acai, and handed one to each of the young missionaries.

Paul, Thomas, Maria, and even Joseph had a tear in their eye. All learned more of the true meaning of Christmas that evening; it's much more about the gift of giving and the joy that comes from giving of yourself to another. It's about getting on your knees and thanking your Savior for His miraculous birthday, and asking for inspiration. It's about the lessons taught and His sacrifice made for us! These missionaries later worked with the father and mother to help them obtain their marriage license and finally enter into the sanctity of marriage. Over the weeks ahead, this family would also learn more of the many blessings of the gospel of Christ to strengthen the ties that bind families together forever.

※ ※ ※

On Christmas day, Paul was given his first opportunity to call his family in California. "Some here are so sweet and ready for the gospel from the first moment we meet them," he told his family. "For others, it is a longer road. But it seems we only need to introduce the gospel, and the Lord takes it from there. These wonderful, humble people accept the challenge," he said. "Broken families are healed; fathers put away their drug and alcohol habits; mothers become loving caregivers setting aside their own proud, selfish, and unholy desires. Marriages are sealed; children gain respect for their parents as Christ takes root in their lives. The lives of these beautiful people are changed, and they begin to see the world differently as we do our best to teach His gospel."

He worked; he watched; he learned as his Father in Heaven revealed His blueprint for happiness to enlighten the lives of those in need. He saw individuals turn away from their own selfish desires, first to their family, then to reach out to others in the gospel. He witnessed the transformation of their very lives as testimonies of the gospel of Christ blossomed. He shared tears of joy as gospel blessings turned lives around, filled hearts and minds with thankfulness and a happiness they had only imagined. He looked on as families came into full bloom with love and respect for one another.

Paul's mom and dad back home in San Diego, received calls morning, noon, and sometimes in the middle of the night, from many expressing their thankfulness for Paul having opened their eyes to the gospel of Christ and the opportunities life held for them. Of course the expression of their love was all in Portuguese. It was a beautiful thing, nonetheless!

The gospel of Christ was infused into Paul's very soul. "Man's greatest happiness comes from losing himself in the service of others."[2]

By the end of his service, Paul had been a lucky participant in hundreds of changed lives, infused with the gospel of Jesus Christ. This experience cemented his own conversion, with a deep and abiding testimony of the work of the gospel and the plan the Savior has for every soul on earth. He stepped off the plane two years later, shoes full of holes, ragged clothes hanging from his body, a changed man forever. His heart was filled with love for the Brazilian people, love of America, of family and most of all, love of the Lord.

✳ ✳ ✳

Paul returned to college from Brazil just in time for the start of fall baseball camp. He was introduced to an entirely new coaching staff with a new program that didn't include him. The pitching coach informed him, "In my opinion you don't make the cut. There is no room for you in our baseball program." Nevertheless, Coach Law agreed to give him a chance. "You'll be our number eleven pitcher on an eleven man staff. If you decide to stay in the program, don't expect to see much playing time. We just have too many good players, Paul."

Once again he threw himself into the game with a passion, but this time with the maturity that comes from spending two years in the service of something greater than himself. He felt confident that his Father in Heaven was with him and would fulfill His part of the bargain. After all He had told him "all would be well," hadn't He? He thanked Coach Law for the opportunity with the promise, "By the start of the conference season, I will be in the three man starting rotation."

Coach Law smiled. "I appreciate the optimism, Paul. Good luck!" To the shock and astonishment of the entire coaching staff, Paul was the number two starting pitcher by the start of the season and the following year, Conference MVP, again setting records along the way. And finally in the last game of his college career, Coach Law let him hit for the first time in an official college game—"cause pitchers don't hit." He went two for two, his lifetime college batting average forever written in the record books—1000.

✳ ✳ ✳

Even after his college career, there were doubters about Paul as a pitcher. The scout for the New York Yankees put it this way, "You gotta hand it to the kid, he did a hell of job with these college hitters, but then these boys are not professionals. It's his flat delivery, even his velocity and movement in the ball won't save him with professionals."

In an after game dinner, the Mariners scout informed Paul, "I love to watch you pitch, Paul, but you're just too small to compete with the big boys. The GM won't let me sign any pitcher under 6' 2". Sorry, Paul."

As Shakespeare put it, "Though [he] be but little, [he] is fierce."[3] Paul started his first professional game in front of a packed stadium. Family and friends listened to the game on the radio. Everyone was nervous— everyone, except Paul, of course. The entire stadium could have thought he was outmatched, but as always Paul was certain it was the batter who should be quaking in his Nike spikes. He pitched a shutout, breaking five bats along the way as his fastball slid inside on these hitters with a wooden bat in their hands. "It was a beautiful sight," he would say after.

He followed his first game with two more shutouts, then went on to finish his first professional season giving up less than one run per game and winning "Rookie of the Year" honors, followed by a call to be the starting pitcher on opening day for Team USA against Canada in the World Cup.

He had been vindicated. Surrounded by dozens of young boys and girls, pen in hand, they waited with hope in their eyes for their chance at Paul's autograph. It brought a smile to remember the little boy covered in dirt except for a shiny white thumb tucked under two blackened front teeth. His Father in Heaven had more than fulfilled his part of the bargain.

Then one day his career as a professional baseball player took an abrupt and traumatic change in direction. Through a series of heart wrenching events, Paul's vision of what he really wanted out of life shifted, then the clouds parted. His future became crystal clear to him and it no longer included baseball. He declined all further offers to play again.

*Following a "Rookie of the Year" performance in his first*
*professional season, came the call as Team USA's starting pitcher*
*on opening day against Canada in the World Cup.*

✳ ✳ ✳

Life is fleeting. It is not a dress rehearsal and Paul wanted more out of life than baseball. Through his missionary service, he had witnessed how

Jesus Christ changes the lives of so many, and now Paul understood just how much Christ had changed his as well. Success in the world of baseball did not mean success in life. He left the game behind and drove cross-country to ask his girlfriend to marry him. The further he drove, the clearer his vision came into focus. Elizabeth and a family centered on the Savior was what he wanted more than anything else in life. He didn't need time away from home and family, chasing dreams of celebrity or the precarious wasteland of illusion promulgated by the world.

Late that night, in a clandestine plot with her roommates and after a visit to a jeweler friend, he entered Elizabeth's apartment, took a knee, and asked for her hand in marriage. With a bright and ardent smile and sparkle in her eyes, she said yes!

It was now clear what his Father in Heaven had in mind for him all along, when that heaven-sent scripture had let him know, "all will be well." A beautiful wife with a testimony of Christ in her heart, and a family of his own to raise in His gospel. This was the very lesson he had marveled at so many times while on his mission serving the many families he met. He watched in heartfelt gratitude as they transformed their lives and found unbounded happiness in their testimonies of Christ.

That service in Brazil had changed him, and now with the help of the Lord he clearly recognized the path leading to his own happiness. And while Elizabeth was willing to accept any path Paul chose, he stood by his conviction despite the tremendous pressure from powerful men encouraging him to pursue fame, glory, and money. Now he knew in his heart that happiness was not the one found on "Sports Center" but instead the path laid out by his Savior, Jesus Christ.

When the manager of the Oakland A's called one last time to try to convince him otherwise, Paul had the courage to say no. The manager who knew Paul well responded to his conviction, "Good for you, Paul. Good for you!"

※ ※ ※

Like my little boy who asked his Father in Heaven for a lightsaber to kill all the bad guys, we don't always get what we want, but if we serve one another with the love of Christ in our hearts, the Lord will give us what we truly need. And all will be well in our search for happiness. It may not come today. It may not come tomorrow. But whether it is in this life or the next, it will come.

Spencer W. Kimball tells us, "The abundant life is also achieved as we magnify our view of life, expand our view of others, and our own possibilities. Thus the more we follow the teachings of the Master, the more enlarged our perspective becomes. We see many more possibilities for service than we would have seen without this magnification. There is great security in spirituality, and we cannot have spirituality without service!"[4]

The abundant life noted in the scriptures is the spiritual sum derived from multiplying service to others by investment of our talents in God's purposes here on earth. Christ reminds us, "Thou shalt love the Lord thy God. . . . This is the first and great commandment. And the second is like unto it, Thou shalt love thy neighbour as thyself."[5] There can be no real abundance in life unless we stay committed to keeping and carrying out those two great commandments. Unless the way we live our lives draws us closer to our Heavenly Father and to our neighbors, there will be emptiness in our lives. It is frightening to see how the lifestyle of so many today causes them to disengage from their families, their friends, and humanity for a life in hedonistic pursuit of selfish pleasures and materialism. To push aside loyalty to family, to community, and to one another in our pursuit of fleeting moments, indulging selfish pleasures that pass with the night is a tragedy in far too many lives.

It is a modern-day misconception that our families do not need the influence of the Savior in their lives. God's plan for us is manifested through our family. Our lives can be nourished by testimony and watered by faith. The lessons learned through service in Christ can take root in our hearts and become a vibrant part of who we are. I bear personal witness to you that true happiness can be found through the quiet, invisible, loving hand of a mother, the example of a righteous father reaching out to serve a neighbor, all within the comforting, loving arms of the gospel of Jesus Christ.

"Two roads diverged in a wood" said the poet Robert Frost, "and I took the one less traveled by, and that has made all the difference."[6] May we take the road laid out for us by our Savior that after our journey is through we might hear him say: "Well done, thou good and faithful servant."[7]

*Jack Fletcher may be sightless, but he has the heart to feel, the ears to hear, and the eyes to truly see the beauty in the world through the gospel of Jesus Christ.*

# By Their Fruits You
# Shall Know Them

When Jesus walked and talked among men, He spoke in a language easily understood. Whether journeying along the dusty road from Nazareth to Jerusalem, addressing the multitudes along the shores of the Sea of Galilee, or pausing to rest beside Jacob's well in Samaria, He taught in parables—simple stories designed to help our hearts know and feel, our ears to hear, and our eyes to truly see.

Jesus taught kindness and empathetic understanding, for He knew this was the way to change the hearts and minds of men—not through hostility, bigotry, or prejudice. Kindness and understanding is a language both the blind can see and the deaf can hear. Spoken through the love of Christ, it is this language that can bring us all together as followers of our Father in Heaven. As Christ said of his followers, "By their fruits ye shall know them."[1]

※ ※ ※

Our family has lived for many years in a small beach town along the north San Diego coastline. Over the years we have come to call many here our friends. And some have been an inspiration to us, improving our lives and ofttimes our relationship with our Father in Heaven. Jack Fletcher is one of those.

From the beginning, Jack has been like another grandfather to our children. He is a joy to be around, so everyone wants to be around him. Jack has been as good a friend our family has ever had.

After returning home from the Great War in Europe and struggling to rejoin society, Jack lost his sight in a terrible accident. He was left to languish in the pain and despair of losing his eyesight, but also to face the haunting challenges of losing his family who abandoned him after the

145

accident. He was angry, depressed, and unhappy at his loss until a caring friend introduced him to the gospel of Jesus Christ.

Under the sweet comforting hand of Christ, his blindness no longer ruled Jack's life. He learned to focus on others and attended church every Sunday as though he had not a care in the world, smiling with light-hearted jokes to bring joy to all around him.

Our family first learned to love Jack when Anne and our youngest son, Daniel, thirteen at the time, gave Jack a ride each week from his home where he lived alone to visit his wife, DeeDee, at a nearby Alzheimer's care facility. Of course, being blind, Jack could not drive himself, so every Wednesday Jack would hitch a ride with Anne some twenty miles to visit his wife. Jack's first words were always the same, "It's so nice to see you, Daniel." One of the greatest gifts in life is the gift of self-deprecating humor. Jack was a master at it.

As Daniel attended a home school sponsored science class, Anne would take Jack to see his DeeDee. It was often a moving experience for Anne to watch Jack tenderly interact with DeeDee. Some days she barely recognized him and others not at all, but on those days when their world came back to them, it was an inspiration to witness.

On one particular occasion, Anne took Jack to buy shoes for DeeDee. Unable to see them, he pelted Anne and the sales woman with questions on color, sizing, and durability. He used his hands to evaluate the fit and texture of the materials and style. Jack was all about style. After careful evaluation he selected just the right pair of shoes for his DeeDee. Their meeting in the Alzheimer care facility after was a touching and moving experience to be remembered.

❈ ❈ ❈

Jack arrives at the care facility full of anticipation with DeeDee's new shoes in hand.

As he enters the room and feels his way to her Jack tenderly smiles and gives DeeDee his sweetest "Hello!"

There is only the slightest acknowledgement.

Without discouragement Jack kneels down before the bed. He gently helps her sit up to face him. Then with some difficulty slips the new pair of shoes onto her feet.

She stares blindly in his direction disoriented and confused. She doesn't recognize him or know why he has brought her the shoes.

Anne looks on from the corner of the room, watching Jack's loving hands gently try to coax DeeDee into cooperating, but try as he might no amount of gentle persuasion convinces her to stand.

At long last he takes her in his arms. She trembles as he whispers something in her ear.

No recognition yet?

But Jack does not give up. He continues to talk to her ever so sweetly.

Then Jack begins to sing, "I danced with the girl with a hole in her stockin', and her knees kept-a knockin' . . . and we danced by the light of the moon."

It's their song and he softly asks, "Dance with me, DeeDee? Dance with me?"

She smiles fondly at the recollection of days gone by and her face starts to come to life. Finally recognition eases across her countenance. As her mind clears, her eyes light up, an affectionate smile spreads brightly across her face. She puts her hand on his shoulder. Then she stands in her new shoes and they dance. Both of them blind, sharing their special moment together, around and around they go in their own special moment, filling the whole room.

Jack continues to sing his best rendition of "Buffalo Gal." A tender smile spreads wide across his face and they are both lost in a world gone by.

She's back with him. The way she was, smiling at him the way she did, and with a kind word of appreciation she shares her love. Jack reciprocates.

Anne can see DeeDee's admiration reflected in her touching expression. They are both living a lifetime over in these few moments.

It warms Jack inside in comforting waves of shared affection as they dance. For in this moment he feels like one lucky man—he has his DeeDee back.

"This is proof that love can still be ours," he whispers in her ear. Then he kisses her. "I love you, DeeDee."

Anne, the guilty observer, feels and hears the emotion in the halting catch of Jack's voice as he continues to sing and dance with his adorable DeeDee. They are in their own world now, oblivious of all around them, including Anne.

For Jack this is a gift from God and it makes every day spent worrying about her all worthwhile.

"What do the doctors know about the power of love anyway?" he whispers to her, a buoyant smile spreading wide across his face.

But then she begins to grow quiet and Jack can feel the fear growing inside her. He recognizes the signs and knows there is nothing he can do to stop it. The moment will soon be gone.

He tries to fend off the inevitable—to bring her back with a comforting and encouraging touch.

"I will never leave you, DeeDee," he whispers but the moment is gone.

"Who are you?" she cries with a panic in her voice. "Why are you here? I don't know you." She recoils, pushing him away with fright showing in her wide eyes. Luckily Jack can't see them.

It is a touching few moments before DeeDee slips back into her inevitable, distant, private world, leaving Jack behind, alone in his darkness. The thief once again has stolen his DeeDee and there is nothing Jack or anyone else can do about it.

Emotion takes hold of Anne as she sits inconspicuously quiet in the corner watching. Tears roll down her cheeks. *No!* The words shout out inside her. *Not yet! Not now. I can't bear to see you lose her after just these few moments Jack. It isn't fair! It isn't fair to either of you.*

But it is to no avail. DeeDee is lost to him for now.

Resignation finally settles in as Jack steps back. A tear comes to the corner of his eye.

But then Jack's countenance turns hopeful once again, as it always does. A soft smile tugs at the corners of his pursed lips.

Sweetly he tells her, "Until next time then . . . my love!"

❋ ❋ ❋

On a Christmas Eve some years ago, we invited Jack to our annual family Christmas dinner. By then DeeDee had passed away, and Jack had become a welcome and frequent guest in our home.

I picked up Jack at his little home where he lived by himself. It was a dark and stormy night. All the lights in the neighborhood had gone dark when I opened the door to his home. It was ink dark inside.

As always, Jack's first words were, "It's nice to see you, David!"

We stepped outside and I closed his front door behind us, when suddenly he remembered the brownies he had made for our Christmas dinner dessert. He had forgotten them on the kitchen counter and asked, "Would you mind if I went back into the kitchen for them. They are awfully good!"

Of course I agreed to go with him to the kitchen to retrieve the brownies.

As requested, I opened the door to let him back into the home. Blinded by the darkness as we entered the house, I instinctively offered, "Jack, it's pitch black in here. Please, let me take your arm."

Of course like the unthinking clumsy escort I was, I immediately stumbled over the chair, almost falling face-first into a desk. Thankfully Jack caught me before I did any damage to me or the desk.

"You're in my world now, David. Let me help you," Jack cautioned.

He gently guided me through the darkness to the plates of desserts he had made in the blackness of his perpetual night, then guided me back to the comfort of my sight. I've never forgotten that cautious walk through his home, guided by the sure hand of this wonderful man.

As Jack led me through the house in debilitating darkness, I realized for a brief moment just how difficult it would be to go through life without the light to guide the way. He had made these brownies from scratch by himself in the blackness of his permanent night.

After an uneventful drive we arrived safely at our home for Christmas dinner. We had also invited Maxine, who was a bit of a recluse living alone in her own home, her husband long since passed away. She was also a character herself and only agreed to come because Jack would be there. Maxine had been a victim of polio as a young girl and for more than eighty years struggled to walk, first with a cane and now with a walker.

At dinner Maxine spoke of the Christmas present she desired most in all the world, but conceded she didn't expect to see it in this life. "But when I pass through those Pearly Gates, I'm gonna run and run and run some more!" She smiled in recognition of her fondest wish.

To which Jack responded, "Yes, and I'm gonna watch you, and watch you and watch you do it again, Maxine!" Of course we all shared in the sweet and personal laughter that followed between these two and in the long entertaining conversation between Jack and Maxine.

Though blind and old age has taken its toll on much of his body, Jack Fletcher lived like he had the world at his feet. He does not see the hot air balloons floating high over the San Elijo estuary on a Sunday afternoon, nor the spectacular sunset as it settles into the Pacific Ocean off Swami's Beach; he does not see the beautiful springtime flowers as they burst into bloom, still he is filled with the Light of Christ, nonetheless. He doesn't even know what our family looks like, yet he loves us just the same.

Jack Fletcher may no longer see the sun as it rises on a crisp spring morning, illuminating the vibrant greens of the Rancho Santa Fe hillsides after a storm, or the rainbow that follows on a Christmas morning, but he would never trade his precious testimony of the gospel of Jesus Christ, even to regain his sight of the beautiful world around him. Jack may be sightless, but he had the heart to know and feel, the ears to hear, and the eyes to truly see the beautiful springtime of the gospel of Jesus Christ.

✳ ✳ ✳

Each of us can imagine just how difficult it might be for Jack going through life without his eyesight. Moreover, each of us knows someone, who unlike Jack has their eyesight, but nevertheless walks in darkness at noonday.

Jesus spoke frequently of those who have eyes but cannot truly see, hearts but do not know or feel, and ears but cannot hear. Unlike Jack, they may not carry the white cane with the red tip and carefully make their way with the sound of the familiar tap, tap, tap, but blind they surely are nonetheless. Some are blinded by the burdens of life because they have not Christ to lift their souls. Some have been blinded by anger, others by indifference, by revenge, by hate. And some are blinded by ignorance, bigotry, and prejudice.

As Jack put it, "I was surprised by the reaction of many of those around me when I joined The Church of Jesus Christ of Latter-day Saints. I felt 'like bein' a caterpillar in a cocoon. . . . Like somethin' asleep wrapped up in a warm place.'[2] I had always thought these to be my friends, the best friends in all the world. Then one day I awoke to the gospel of Jesus Christ, as though I had awoken from a long sleep to 'become a butterfly' in the springtime of my life. I was happier, more content and more fulfilled than ever before; it was a choice that helped me to forget myself, my troubles and instead focus on helping others and the work that had to be done. Living the gospel of Christ opened the door to opportunities I never even knew existed. It led me to my wife, my soul mate," Jack shared. "But I was no longer welcome with some, unless I left my new found religion at the door."

"Your doctrine is different than ours now, Jack," he was told. "We cannot accept your church in the circle of our Christian community or invite you into our Christian associations."

Jack would say of those disappointing times, "It didn't make no sense to me, but then you can't tell a bumblebee he can't fly, can you? So what could I do? I had knelt in prayer time and again, poured out my heart and soul to my Father in Heaven and I knew in my heart and down in the very depths of my soul this gospel was true. There was nothing I could do to change that. More importantly, it made me happy. It made me a better man. I was more involved in improving the lives of others, spending less time worrying about myself. So what could I do?"

What are any of us to do if some around us deny the changes for good they see in our lives? Changes they can see with their own eyes and hear with their own ears, but refuse to acknowledge the Christian lives of those living in their midst. What should any good Christian do when criticized for their faith? After all, most of us like Jack are unwilling participants in the stand to defend our faith against an outgoing cultural tide, but here we are as brothers and sisters in Christ nonetheless. So what do we do?

All any of us can do, really, is to continue to struggle daily to live our lives in concert with the commandments of God and to continue to try within the limits of our human frailty to believe Christ. To believe in the love of God and the principals His gospel shares with each of us on the strength of families, faith, hope, and charity, and to offer our gratitude for our many blessings received from our Savior.

Christians are rarely called upon to be the good Christian in a difficult situation, but when we are, we should be thankful to have men like Jack Fletcher to show us the way to respond to a criticism of our faith.

"Kill 'em with kindness," Jack would tell us.

As the Apostle Paul urged, "Be thou an example of the believers."[3] For as Christ said of His followers, "By their fruits ye shall know them."[4]

In a recent press release from The Church of Jesus Christ of Latter-day Saints, an expression of the beliefs for members of our faith was given: "[We] believe in the Jesus of the Bible, the same that was born at Bethlehem, grew up in Nazareth, preached His gospel in Galilee and Judea, healed the sick, raised the dead, and finally offered Himself as a sinless ransom for the sins of the world. They believe that Jesus Christ was literally resurrected, that He lives today, and that He is the only name under heaven by which mankind can be saved. This is the Jesus whose name is depicted on the front of every Mormon place of worship. This is the Jesus in whose name every Mormon prays and every sermon is preached. This is the Jesus whose body and blood are commemorated in weekly worship services by Latter-day Saints from Nigeria to New Zealand, from Michigan to Mongolia."[5]

Must we not believe the Lord when he says, the Spirit of Christ is given to every man, for "every spirit that confesseth that Jesus Christ is come in the flesh is of God."[6] As Jack would put it, "There may be differences in our beliefs that elude us, but we have more in common to bring us together, than in our differences that divide us." And like Jack who had never even seen his DeeDee in this life, we can love completely even though we may not completely know or understand each other.

It is a beautiful day, like no other, to be a follower of Jesus Christ. Let the world witness firsthand the spirit and testimonies of those who represent their faith by the way they live their lives. It is the language of kindness and gentle persuasion that the deaf can hear and the blind can see. There is no greater power of persuasion to convince mankind of our Christianity than through the hearts and spirits of those who constantly strive to choose the right.

Let others see for themselves who you are through your own actions and patient longsuffering sharing of Christ's message, "Neither do men light a candle, and put it under a bushel, but on a candlestick; and it giveth light unto all that are in the house,"[7] Christ said. "I am the light of the world: he that followeth me shall not walk in darkness, but shall have the light of life."[8] "And you will know them by their fruits."[9]

During this Christmas season may our light so shine that we glorify our Heavenly Father. Let us each resolve that over this coming year, we will take the opportunity to demonstrate our faith in the birth, life, and Atonement of Jesus Christ to all mankind. Let all those who are willing, use their eyes to see with and ears to hear with, and then touch and feel for themselves the healing power of the gospel of Christ. And let the kindness and understanding begin with us . . . with me and with you.

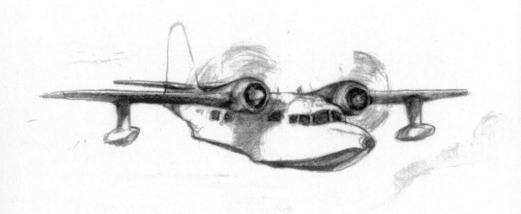

*The throbbing hum of the powerful twin engines beneath our
wings numbed my mind into a blissful trance of daydreams.
It was a peaceful way to pass a late summer afternoon.*

# Man Is That He Might Have Joy

*I* first stepped onto the university campus, totally and completely unprepared for the experience that was about to unfold before me. The first in a long line of family to attend a higher education of any kind, I knew little of college life, and even less of the institution that supported it. I was young, self-absorbed, and had a head full of mush, and I suppose my quiet demeanor led many to suspect an ignorant arrogance in me and I'm sure for some, when I did speak, it removed all doubt.

I had been invited to attend university for one reason and for one reason only—solely because I could get from one end of the swimming pool to the other very, very quickly. And from the beginning, I crossed my fingers in the hope they wouldn't find me out and rescind the invitation.

I can tell you now, though I tried my best to deny it then, my heart was touched by the sweet testimony of a remarkable young co-ed unlike anyone I had ever met before, or since frankly. I still don't know how I talked that beautiful young woman into consenting to be my wife. She took a big risk marrying a reprobate like me, especially outside of the gospel. For as my children are often kind enough to remind me, I had grown up ghetto—a cultural catastrophe, having spent more of my ill-spent youth shooting pool in Grandma's Saloon, than in my dysfunctional and tumultuous home, stuck in the middle of a brutal neighborhood without the calming influence of a stable family, or the soothing confidence of a Christian upbringing. We were poor in both the things of the world and of the spirit. It left all of us in my family with emotional scars, and me with a driving insecurity to do whatever necessary to achieve that Great American Dream no matter the cost.

Anne . . . well, Anne was everything I wasn't. I was hardly deserving of her unwavering devotion and clear vision of the world that the Gospel afforded her. But I didn't see it then. I was blinded by my only remarkable attribute—a passionate determination to avoid the life sentence of drudgery that I so often witnessed while growing up in the Heights. In my mind I knew, if only I could parlay an education into my ticket out, well . . . then life would be awesome. No church was gonna stand in the way of my pursuit of happiness.

In time, after many long days on very short purse strings, I graduated with an exceptional education in engineering and business, built a thriving business with an impressive home in the most exclusive neighborhood of Santa Monica, California—with a sweet little point break just down the beach. Celebrities of every kind lived in our midst. I was not yet thirty, with a beautiful wife, inside and out, a young son, and another on the way. I suppose, in the eyes of the world, I was indeed a success in life, or at least I appeared to be.

I thought myself too busy. Too busy to make the family my priority. Too busy to burden myself with Church obligations. Too busy, with more important things in life.

Then one summer's day, it all changed.

※ ※ ※

I had a project under construction on Catalina Island and took a small commercial seaplane to and from the island. I had made that flight many times, but on this particular day, for the very first time, I was invited by the captain to join him in the cockpit on the flight back to the mainland. It was an offer I couldn't refuse.

As I sat in the copilot's seat, I was impressed by the view through the Plexiglas windshield that encapsulated the entire cockpit. A 270-degree, panoramic view of the ocean spread out before me. It was a beautiful sight.

We taxied down the runway ramp and into the water. I felt the bump of the water on the pontoons, under a slight breeze accompanying that warm summer afternoon and the rumble of the idling engines. I noticed the salt encrusted side window that would not close all the way, and wondered just how carefully the FAA monitored these old vintage World War II planes.

Then, suddenly the pilot pulled the stick toward him, and the exhilarating surge of centrifugal force, thrust me back into my seat. Adrenaline rushed through my veins as the powerful twin engines accelerated beneath our wings. We skipped and bounced across the textured surface until finally, we lifted into the air—banking through a wide arc, toward the Long Beach Airport some thirty minutes away.

The sun glistened off the surface of the pale green Catalina Harbor. Dozens of billowing white sails on majestic sailboats below bloomed in striking contrast to the brilliant-blue sky overhead. Startled buffalo loped up the mountain slopes as we climbed above Wrigley Peak, giving way to a horizon filled with seemingly endless open ocean.

We turned easterly, leaving the island behind. Flocks of pelicans skimmed the surface just past the surf line. Pods of great white sharks basking in the warmth of the summer sun scattered along the surface of the open ocean. Schools of dolphin playing their game of "chase me if you can" encircled the fishing boats heading back to port for the evening.

As we drew nearer the mainland, the setting sun eased into the western horizon. The throbbing hum of the powerful twin engines beneath our wings had numbed my mind into a blissful trance of daydreams. It was a peaceful way to pass a late summer afternoon.

Then, just as we passed over the breakwater buffering the Long Beach shoreline, the late afternoon calm was shattered by a loud pop, then a tensiled snap, on the left side of the plane. The plane had blown an engine, damaging a vital aileron controlling the lift of the wings. We violently shook, shuttered, and jerked left, plummeting earthward in a spiral free-fall. I pressed back into my flight seat as we fell, gripping it with fear, in a pathetically helpless attempt to stop the plane from falling. My heart lodged in my throat. A thick trail of black smoke stretched out behind us. The remaining engine whined in such a high-pitched howl, I thought it might break apart. The pilot struggled to right the falling plane, his eyes the size of saucers and his hands shaking badly; it seemed clear to me he was even more afraid than I was. I felt totally and entirely helpless.

I took a quick breath and with my heart pounding, I glanced through the cabin porthole separating us from the passengers. I saw my partner and the rest of the passengers looking back at me—frantic, terrified, desperate for answers.

I turned away, and ignored them all.

Finally, somehow, the pilot pulled us out of our free-fall. But we had lost what precious little altitude we had. Well off course now and well inland, San Pedro's dense residential neighborhoods stretched out below us. The pilot called into the airport. The air traffic controller assured him they would clear the runway. "Just do what you need to do to get the plane down, and we will have emergency vehicles and an ambulance there waiting."

Hardly reassuring! We awkwardly limped in toward the airport, dropping in elevation as we went.

Then the pilot uttered words that will forever have a special home in my memory, "We can't make the airport."

As the cliché suggests, my life did indeed pass before my very eyes, but the meetings, projects, and business deals, that seemed so important just moments ago, none of it mattered now. Funny, what popped into my head was an obscure regret. I wished I had gone to church with my family on Sunday.

I bowed my head to say a little prayer. "Father in Heaven, if this is a test, you've got my attention. I want to see my beautiful wife again. I want to be there for the birth of our baby boy. I want to watch my son Michael grow to be a man." I promised my Father in Heaven if he would get me through this, I would do whatever it was He might want me to do.

Aldous Huxley wrote, "Most human beings have an almost infinite capacity for taking things for granted"[1]—for not recognizing what is really most important in life. And frankly, I had been no exception.

Now, dangerously low, I could see shocked faces in the car windows below. The pilot, scouting the horizon, turned toward the harbor that seemed our only sanctuary. We whisked over the scattered docks, and through the jungle of structures on every side. So low now—I could read the lips of a fisherman in the harbor below. I won't tell you what he said.

The Vincent Thomas Bridge loomed large before us as we approached at what seemed a blistering speed. I knew we were going to slam right into it. Then, in a moment that seemed like a lifetime, the sky—so blue, so clear, so beautiful—opened up beneath the bridge and we slipped under it, bumped on the surface of the water, landed in the harbor, settling safely between two large freighters docked for portage.

A pool of dark black oil oozed out in a circle from around our little plane as it bobbed serenely in the calm quiet of the harbor water.

The crisis over, my hands began to shake uncontrollably. I wiped my eyes, then the sweat from my face. I hugged my family tight that night. I thanked my Father in Heaven. We went to church as a family that Sunday.

※ ※ ※

Sometimes, even with the gospel of Christ ringing in our ears, we misuse our God-given agency to follow priorities set by the world, and displace the most important things in life. We foolishly follow a world that, as Isaiah predicted, "call[s] evil good, and good evil; that put[s] darkness for light, and light for darkness."[2]

In this our twenty-first century, misguided politicians, terrorists, environmental alarmists, and "Gadianton Robbers" of our freedoms and liberty, would have us "worship the creature, but defile the man and his creator,"[3] as the apostle Paul prophesied of our time, more than two thousand years ago. These mists of darkness descend on all travelers, the faithful and determined ones as well as the weak and ungrounded ones. It is only the gospel of Christ, infused into our lives, that enlightens us with the power of discernment. This clarifying force entering the very veins of our soul, helps us reconcile and make sense of the world around us.

To quote Jeffrey R. Holland, "Love. Healing. Help. Hope. The power of Christ to counter all troubles in all times"[3]—including our time. He is a safe harbor from the distractions of the world, which would lure us down forbidden paths, with taunts to "come follow me" the unrighteous, into misery, heartache, and despair. However dark or difficult the journey, that rod of the gospel marks the way of the solitary redeeming trail in our pursuit of happiness, and returns us to our Eternal Heavenly Father, who loves us deeply.

※ ※ ※

A few short weeks after our crash landing, my partner, Al Coluzzi, was on PSA, flight 182, when it fell from the sky and crashed approaching Lindbergh Field. My partner and all 144 passengers and crew were killed.

I sat at Al's funeral, watching his wife and two boys, suffering the terrible anguish of loss, without the comforting balm of the gospel of Christ in their lives. What a plight, wondering if her husband, and frankly every man, woman, and child in this life was free falling to permanent death, spiritually plummeting toward eternal anguish. As Jeffrey Holland asks, "Is that what life was meant to be? Is that the grand finale of the human experience?" Is life pointless? Is everything and everyone we love meaningless? Are we all to be jettisoned to some cold, dark eternity of nothingness in an indifferent universe, with nothing but the feeling of helplessness as we tightly grip our flight seat through life, nothing to save us, nothing we can do to land safely, much less someone to carry us safely home? Is our only purpose in life an empty existential exercise? To simply drift through life for a few decades, then free fall into oblivion?

Jeffrey R. Holland's answer to those questions is "an unequivocal and eternal no!"[4] It is Christ who is the light and the way to our salvation and eternal life. This is the reason we celebrate Christ, His birth, His teachings, His Atonement. From the moment our first parents stepped out of the Garden of Eden, God, the father of us all, declared that this entire sequence of life was designed for our own eternal happiness. It was part of His Divine Plan all along, to provide a Savior, the very son of God Himself, who would come in the meridian of time to atone for our transgressions. That Atonement would achieve complete victory over physical death, unconditionally granting resurrection to every person who has ever been born or ever will be born into this world. Mercifully with our choice

*PSA flight 182 fell from the sky and crashed, killing my partner and all 144 passengers and crew.*

to repent of our sins and follow His commandments, Christ's Atonement also provides forgiveness for the personal sins of all of us, from Adam to the end of the world. His divine forgiveness extends to you and to me, for God knows we need it, don't we?

✳ ✳ ✳

After my life-changing calamity, reaffirmed by the tragedy of Al's funeral, I took a lot less for granted. This powerful tragedy had left me shaken, but with a clearer understanding of the loss and level of intense heartbreak suffered by so many.

As promised, I covenanted with the Lord to change the focus of my life, even if it meant giving up on my own pursuit of personal happiness. And with the Lord's help, I tried to be good to my word. I tried to do what I thought my Father in Heaven would want me to do, what Christ through His birth, life and sacrifice has asked all of us to do.

I opened my heart, allowed His Gospel into my life, and made it a priority to support my family in it. Surprisingly, I suppose for the first time really, I felt Christ's Atoning influence in my life. And as the story is told, time and again in the scriptures, I began the long journey toward a mighty change of heart to be born again in Christ. A life-changing quest, not as the world would suggest from the outside in, rather as the gospel changes lives, from the inside-out.

In time, I knelt across the altar of the temple, was sealed to my beautiful wife for time and all eternity, and with tears of unfettered joy and happiness streaming down my face, watched my two little boys being escorted into that sealing room, uncharacteristically quiet, with a look of wonderment spread wide across their little faces. Faces I will never forget as long as I live. At that moment, there was no question in my mind why my Savior was born, lived, and died for us. There was no question about what was most important in life—my devoted Anne, fatherhood, my Savior. I knew then what real joy and happiness felt like, and I knew what my Savior meant when he said, "I am the light of the world,"[5] the comforting balm that warms the heart. I testify to you of the truthfulness of the scripture: "For what is a man profited, if he shall gain the whole world, and lose his own soul"[6] and family? I had set aside my personal pursuit of happiness—only to find it.

So many of us—lost souls in the world—need to be found. We live our lives, concerned about things that in the long run, really don't matter much at all—do they? We're caught up in the thick of thin things, because we can't see who we really are: literal sons and daughters of our Father in Heaven. We need only allow the gospel of Christ to enlighten our vision of the world around us, that we might really live life to the fullest. "Happiness is the meaning and purpose of life, the whole aim and end of human existence, and will be there for us, if we but pursue the right path that leads to it."[7]

Don't place the foundation for your life upon the shifting sands of popular opinion in a secular world, where the philosophies of men have rendered fatherhood a lost art and decimated the family. Instead, place your life and family—with all your hopes, with all your dreams—in the pierced hands of your Savior. Have the courage to stand strong against the ever-changing chorus of humanity, for a virtuous life. Focus on the gospel rudder. Ignore the turbulence of life. Listen to the still small voice that enlightens your soul's ability to discern your course through life, and land safely at your heavenly destination. It will touch your very soul and is the passport to peace and happiness in your life.

I bear my personal testimony of these principles, and promise you, if you but do your best to follow the teachings of Jesus Christ and the prophets, you will be filled with love, with peace, and with the happiness that we all seek. May I be a witness that God lives, that Jesus Christ was born, lived, and died for us, and that through Him we can find our own personal happiness.

# Notes

## The Great Christmas Train Ride

This story is substantially true, except that the events of the train ride occurred over two separate occasions: Christmas 1968 and Thanksgiving 1970. I was not alone on the train rides but with Darren Wester on the first train ride and Noel Laverty on the second. In addition, Annie did not make it back home until the day after Christmas.

Interestingly, my great-great-grandfather Thomas Wright with his new wife, Annie Dale, and brother Joseph immigrated by clipper ship from Yorkshire England to America, wagon train to Wyoming, then worked building the Union Pacific Trans-Continental Railroad in 1868–69, finishing at Promontory Point for the driving of the golden spike by Leland Stanford on May 10, 1869.

Most of the Wright family settled along the Wyoming border before it had become a state, with the rest of the family joining Thomas in Wyoming the following year. His mother, Martha, father, Joseph, and sister immigrated from England, arriving on one of the first Trans-continental train rides in 1870 and 1874, respectively.

1. Mark Twain, *Life on the Mississippi* (New York: Harpers & Brothers Publishers, 1911), 414.
2. Author unknown. Commonly attributed to George Carlin or Hilary Cooper.
3. John 13:34–35; emphasis added.
4. Thomas S. Monson, "A Doorway Called Love," *Ensign*, Nov. 1987.

## Skate Rising

This story is inspired by true events. There was some license in portraying the Holiday Skate, and some names were changed to preserve their privacy. Skate Rising is growing daily and now advocates and supports many other worthy causes around the world with events over California. Skate Rising supports a community of young girls lifting each other to greater heights while serving one another and those in need with unconditional love.

1. Author unknown. Often attributed to Winston Churchill or Abraham Lincoln.

## Angels in Their Midst

The story is based on true events, although for the flow of the story, I didn't let the conversations or details get in the way.

1. Attributed to Henry Ford.

2. Variation of a quote attributed to William Arthur Ward: "Feeling gratitude and not expressing it is like wrapping a present and not giving it."
3. Harriet Beecher Stowe, published as Christopher Crowfield, *Little Foxes* (Boston: Ticknor and Fields, 1866).

## SERVE ONE ANOTHER

The story and events are true, though some of the names have been changed and Emma and Abby were added.

1. Galations 5:13
2. Mark 8:35
3. Matthew 25:34–36
4. Matthew 25:37–39
5. Matthew 25:40

## THE SPIRIT OF CHRISTMAS

The theme of the story is taken from a Thomas S. Monson Christmas message.

1. Thomas S. Monson, First Presidency Christmas devotional, December 7, 2008. See also Luke 2:7.
2. Luke 2:7
3. Luke 2:13
4. Thomas S. Monson, First Presidency Christmas Devotional, 2008.
5. Luke 9:58
6. Thomas S. Monson, "The Gifts of Christmas," *Ensign*, December 2003.
7. Aldous Huxley, "Variations on a Philosopher," in *Themes and Variations* (1950).
8. Matthew 27:42
9. Luke 23:34
10. Luke 23:46
11. Isaiah 41:10
12. Psalm 30:5
13. Thomas S. Monson, First Presidency Christmas Devotional, 2008.
14. 1 Chronicles 28:9
15. Attributed to Ralph Waldo Emerson.
16. Thomas S. Monson, "The Spirit of Christmas," *Ensign*, December 1993.
17. Thomas S. Monson, "My Redeemer Lives," *Ensign*, February 2001.
18. Thomas S. Monson, "Because He Came," Church broadcast, December 2001, https://www.lds.org/broadcasts/article/christmas-devotional/2011/12/because-he-came.

## THE BIGGEST, BADDEST, MAD DOG IN TOWN

The events of the story are true and the characters are real persons, although the conversation was created and some details added to keep the flow of the story and connect events. Of course, David is the boy of my youth.

1. *The Rookie* (1990), directed by Clint Eastwood.
2. Harry Emerson Fosdick, *Living under Tension: Sermons on Christianity Today* (1941).

3. Theodore Roosevelt, "Citizenship in a Republic," a speech at the Sorbonne, Paris, France (23 April 1910).
4. Jeffrey R. Holland, "An High Priest of Good Things to Come," *Ensign*, Nov. 1999. Narrative referenced and reconfigured with emphasis added to fit the story.

## RACHEL'S CHOICE
The story of Sadie and family relationships are based on true events with modifications to fit the theme of the story on Christmas morning.

1. Thomas S. Monson
2. Charles Dickens, *A Christmas Carol.*
3. Proverbs 20:12
4. 1 Samuel 16:7
5. Acts 9:15–16
6. Acts 9:6, with emphasis
7. John 3:5
8. 2 Corinthians 12:7–9
9. 1 Corinthians 1:27
10. Peace prayers, St. Joan of Arch, with modification and emphasis.
11. Jeffrey R. Holland, "The First Great Commandment," *Ensign*, Nov. 2012.

## CHRISTMAS TRADITIONS
The stories are true, but time is consolidated for the purpose of the narrative.

1. Attributed to Mark Twain.
2. Matthew 22:39
3. John 13:34
4. Thomas S. Monson, "Finding Joy in the Journey," *Ensign*, November 2008.
5. From *The Music Man*, as quoted in Monson, "Finding Joy in the Journey."
6. Thomas S. Monson, "Dedication Day," *Ensign*, November 2000.

## HIS CHRISTMAS GIFT
The story is true. Jeff and his wife Kjerstin are raising a beautiful family with three children, and his parents are living close by, enjoying their grandchildren and the blessings of the gospel in their lives.

1. John 9:25
2. Pierre Teilhard De Chardin, in *The Phenomenon of Man* [*Le Phénomène Humain*] (1955).
3. Neal A. Maxwell, as quoted by David A. Bednar, "Things as They Really Are," *Ensign*, June 2010.
4. Psalm 46:10
5. Winston Churchill, "Never Give In" (speech), Harrow School, October 29, 1941.
6. John 8:12

## NEVER A FINER CHRISTMAS

The events in the story are true, except my father died on a Sunday in the fall of 2005. Leron Lee later played centerfield for the San Diego Padres and his son Derek Lee will someday be in the Hall of Fame.

1. Attributed to Ralph Waldo Emerson.
2. Sarah Ban Breathnach, as quoted at quotationsbook.com/quote/17776.
3. Russell M. Nelson, "Doors of Death," *Ensign*, May 1992.
4. Isaiah 41:10
5. Thomas S. Monson, "I Know that My Redeemer Lives!" *Ensign*, May 2007.
6. Hebrews 9:27
7. Luke 23:46
8. Isaiah 41:10
9. Psalm 30:5
10. Harriet Beecher Stowe, published as Christopher Crowfield, *Little Foxes* (Boston: Ticknor and Fields, 1866).
11. John 3:16

## THE THIN LINE BETWEEN GIVER AND RECEIVER

1. John 11:25–26

## FAMILIES ARE FOREVER

The story is true, both for Michael and Paul.

1. John Greenfield Whittier, "Maud Muller" (1856).
2. Psalm 127:3
3. "The Family: A Proclamation to the World," *Ensign* or *Liahona*, November 2010, 129.
4. Mark 8:36
5. Harold B. Lee, *Strengthening the Home* (1973), 7.
6. David O. McKay, in Conference Report, April 1964, 5.
7. Proverbs 22:6

## THE ROAD LESS TRAVELED

The events in this story are true. The Christmas event is, however, a composite of various families and events.

1. Isaiah 41:10
2. David O. McKay, in Conference Report, October 1963, 8.
3. William Shakespeare, *A Midsummer Night's Dream*, act 3, scene 2.
4. Spencer W. Kimball, "The Abundant Life," *Ensign*, July 1978.
5. Matthew 22:36–39
6. Robert Frost, "The Road Not Taken," st. 4 (1916).
7. Matthew 25:21

## A Christmas for Sadie

The story is true. Sadie has done very well in the intervening years, graduating from Santa Fe Christian High School and earning a college degree. She plans to help other foster children and have a family of her own.

1. John 15:13
2. Matthew 22:39
3. *Shenandoah*, directed by Andrew V. McLaglen (1965), as quoted in Thomas S. Monson, "They Pray and They Go," *Ensign*, May 2002.
4. Mosiah 2:17

## By Their Fruits You Shall Know Them

The stories are true, although some license was taken in the interaction between individuals. Jack Fletcher passed away in 2016 and many, many of all faiths were there at his memorial to celebrate his life, including some from the political class since Jack had been the advocate for the blind to the California State Legislature, appointed by Governor Ronald Reagan. There were several testimonials of the inspiration he left each of us in our lives.

1. Matthew 7:20
2. Harper Lee, *To Kill a Mockingbird* (J. B. Lippincott & Co., 1960).
3. 1 Timothy 4:12
4. Matthew 7:20
5. Michael Otterson, "Are Mormons Christians?" *OnFaith*, December 10, 2007.
6. 1 John 4:2
7. Matthew 5:15
8. John 8:12
9. Matthew 7:16

## Man Is That He Might Have Joy

The story is true with one exception—the timing of Anne's pregnancy with Paul. Some months after the crash landing of the seaplane an engine blew again. This time it was during take off. The seaplane flipped, crashed, and two passengers were killed. PSA 182 to San Diego crashed in 1978 killing 144, including my colleague Al Coluzzi. Both PSA and the seaplane airlines went out of business as results of their respective fatal crashes.

1. Aldous Huxley, "Variations on a Philosopher" in *Themes and Variations* (1950).
2. Isaiah 5:20
3. Jeffrey R. Holland, "Safety for the Soul," *Ensign*, November 2009.
4. Jeffrey R. Holland, "Where Justice, Love, and Mercy Meet," *Ensign*, May 2015.
5. John 8:12
6. Matthew 16:26
7. Attributed to Aristotle.

# Acknowledgments

*I* would like to offer a special acknowledgment and thanks to Kiyomi Fukui, who spent long, loving hours drawing and redrawing sketches for this book, never complaining, always cheerful, and just a joy to work with on this project.

I would also like to thank my dear friend Patricia McGeeney for the painting she so graciously gave my family for this book.

I would like to thank my friends Perter Stern and many others for suggesting I write this book and Marilyn Faulkner that I publish it with Cedar Fort, who have been very helpful and patient in helping me put it together.

Finally, I would like to acknowledge all those who inspired the stories told within these pages: Anne Gray Jacinto, Calli and Matt Kelsay, Kevin Smith, David and Melissa Drake, Sadie Knox, Dolores Eileen and Alvin Jacinto, Paul and Constance Ray, Brent Toolson, John Ek, Jerry Crickmore, John Fausnaut, Paul Heron, Michael Jacinto, Paul Jacinto, Elizabeth Jacinto, Rachel Jacinto, Daniel Jacinto, Sadie, Helen Woodward, Jeff Yates, Jim and Jody Yates, Albert Bertha, Stephanie Gwilliam, Leron Lee, Ryan Flaherty, Tony Gwynn, Jack Fletcher, Al Coluzzi, and Marsha Tudor.

# About the Author

avid A. Jacinto was born into a family living on the wrong side of the tracks and has been a storyteller ever since, some true and some not so much so. He retired from a very successful business life, often interjecting colorful stories in his many speaking engagements, some drawn from his ill-spent youth while growing up in the California of the 1950s and '60s, an entirely different world than exists today. Others are entertaining and humorous exposés on the challenges of growing into a successful and productive adult, or the trials of parenting, where, as he puts it, "I learned of the beauty and unmatched love that comes from some modicum of success in that sacred vocation." He supposes his greatest achievement was being lucky enough to talk the fetching Anne Gray into marrying him, fortunate enough to grow up with his four beautiful children, and blessed enough to have seven near-perfect grandchildren.